6996

940.54 Markl, Julia
MAR
     The Battle of
     Britain

12.00
~~$11.90~~
                     6996

| ~~NOV 3 0 1991~~ DATE | | |
|---|---|---|
| ~~OCT 1 3 1992~~ | | |
| | | |
| | | |
| | | |
| | | |
| | | |
| | | |
| | | |
| | | |

# WWII

## THE BATTLE OF BRITAIN

# WORLD

# TURNING POINTS OF

# THE BATTLE OF BRITAIN

## JULIA MARKL

FRANKLIN WATTS ▪ 1984
NEW YORK ▪ LONDON ▪ TORONTO ▪ SYDNEY

Photographs courtesy of:
Culver Pictures, Inc.: pp. 11, 14, 86, 91, 96;
AP/Wide World: pp. 33, 83; UPI: p. 45;
Air Ministry, London: p. 55;
Imperial War Museum: pp. 61, 68;
The Bettmann Archive: p. 71.

Map courtesy of Vantage Art, Inc.

Library of Congress Cataloging in Publication Data

Markl, Julia.
The Battle of Britain

(Turning points of World War II)
Includes bibliographical references and index.
Summary: Traces the events that led to the attempted
German invasion of Great Britain in 1940 describing the
prolonged bombing of London by the Luftwaffe, the tactical
errors made by the Germans, and how the outcome of the
battle affected the course of the war.
1. Britain, Battle of, 1940—Juvenile literature.
[1. Britain, Battle of, 1940-      2. World War,
1939-1945—Great Britain]  I. Title.  II. Series.
D756.5.B7M28 1984              940.54′21              84-7396
ISBN 0-531-04861-6

# CONTENTS

To one who taught me to fly
and one who taught me to
believe in myself.

# INTRODUCTION

Dunkirk, the French coast, May 27–June 4, 1940. Five hundred thousand British, French, and Belgian troops had been forced to a last stand in what seemed to be total defeat. On a seven-mile perimeter they faced the overwhelming odds of three German panzer divisions—composed of the same German tanks that had cut through France and Belgium in less than a month—and from the air the Allies suffered constant bombing and strafing by the Luftwaffe.

They had retreated as far as possible. At their backs lay the English Channel. In some places only twenty miles wide, that strip of sea stretched between the Allied armies and safety. The Channel, which had foiled all invasions of Britain since William the Conqueror in 1066, kept five hundred thousand men on the beach at Dunkirk . . . and the best evacuation plans assured the rescue of only forty-five thousand. Almost the entire professional army of Britain was about to be swallowed up, killed, or captured with their weapons by the victorious Germans.

Never had Hitler's armies seemed so invincible; never had the Allied cause seemed so hopeless. Czechoslovakia, Poland, Holland, Denmark, Norway—all had been overrun in the past nine months. Belgium had surrendered to the same German divisions that the Allies now faced. France, thought to have the greatest army in the world, and Britain, with the world's most powerful navy protecting its far-flung dominions, seemed threatened with total defeat by a country that had been at their mercy twenty years earlier.

The beaches of Dunkirk were thick with men awaiting transport. Standing offshore in deep water were the evacuation ships. There was no way the navy could provide enough small boats to carry the waiting soldiers from the beach. But from all the southeast coast of England came fishing boats, barges, motor launches, and sailboats—requisitioned, commandeered, volunteered for this duty. It was an incredible flotilla that included an America's Cup racing yacht, a former gunboat that had seen service on the Yangtze River in China, a paddle-wheel minesweeper, ferry boats, and a variety of craft, from humble fishing boats under sail to an armed luxury yacht complete with its noble owner and his personal chef. Some were piloted by sailors of the Royal Navy, but many were personally handled by their owners—fishermen, lords, and other civilians. Added to these craft were improvisations from the beach, such as a raft made from a door, which carried out three Belgians and a Frenchman. For a week hundreds of small craft came through waters made treacherous by mines, finding their way without lighted navigation buoys or lightships because these had been blacked out to reduce chances of attack by the German air force.

That air force, the Luftwaffe, was ruthlessly and efficiently harrying the Allies both at sea and on shore. Stukas—single-engine dive-bombers—plunged, screaming, the sirens on their wings meant to increase the terror of the beleaguered army below. But the soldiers remained calm even as German shore artillery delivered round after round into the steadily shrinking Allied enclave and into the busy sea.

The small boats plowed ceaselessly back and forth with their five or fifteen or fifty rescued men. Many were taken from the beach only to die, with their rescuers, in the water. Thousands of trips were made from the beach to the waiting ships, guided by smoke by day and fire by night, as the town of Dunkirk burned along with the fuel tanks that had supplied the harbor. The oily smoke became a blessing as it lay its protective pall between the crowded beach and the marauding Stukas.

Despite the numbers, the strafing, the lack of protective cover—all invitations to panic—the withdrawal was orderly. The men stood in lines from the beaches out into the water; waist deep, chin deep, they waited their turn to climb into the next boat. One sixteen-year-old, Robert Elvins, who had talked his way onto one of the rescue boats at Greenwich as replacement for an injured crew member, said his captain got angry when too many men tried to get into the craft. They were climbing in from all sides in spite of his shouts, so he picked up a spanner and shook it at them, saying, "Act like Englishmen, can't you, and wait your turn! Or do I have to take this to you?" One of the men replied, "How can I act like an Englishman when I'm a bloody Welshman?" But they began to laugh, and enough of them dropped back into the sea. The boat managed to do good work, although it was sunk twice and had to be beached and repaired. The Stukas dive-bombed and strafed, and those on board would duck below deck. They would come up on deck to find the sea full of soldiers' bodies and the water so bloody that it stained those who still lived to climb into the boat.

Out on the mole, a breakwater to which larger ships could tie to take on men, the soldiers waited three abreast. Time after time they had to throw themselves flat as the enemy planes approached, gunfire stitching a pattern across the water and into their ranks.

Many a man looked up and wondered where the Royal Air Force could be, for British planes of the RAF were seldom seen. They were, in fact, there, above the smoke and clouds. The Spitfires and Hurricanes would cross the Channel and engage the enemy, inflicting tolls of four to one on the Germans. But too much fuel was used getting to the battle area, so the engagements were short. Their pilots' heroism was not as visible as that of the men below—the soldiers, the sailors, and the civilians who joined them in the rescue, and the rear guard, French and British, which protected the retreat and whose men were not themselves able to escape.

Winston Churchill, the British prime minister, warned Parliament and the world that the "miracle" of Dunkirk was not a victory. "Wars," he said, "are not won by evacuation." But, he assured the world on June 4, 1940:

> We shall not flag or fail. We shall go on to the end. We shall fight in France, we shall fight on the seas and oceans, we shall fight with growing confidence and growing strength in the air. We shall defend our island, whatever the cost may be, we shall fight on the beaches, we shall fight on the landing grounds, we shall fight in the fields and in the streets, we shall fight in the hills. We shall never surrender.

And on June 18, following the surrender by the French to the Germans, he said:

> The Battle of France is over. The Battle of Britain is about to begin . . . Hitler knows he will have to break us in this island or lose the war.

Miraculous as the rescue at Dunkirk was—over three hundred thousand British and French soldiers were taken off the beaches in that week—there would be more to the story than bravery and determination. And the story began long before Dunkirk.

To see the Battle of Britain as a turning point in World War II, you must look at the direction of events before the Battle and then at how that direction changed after the Battle. Go back all the way to 1919.

World War I, "the war to end all wars," had just ended, and the Allies intended that name to be a reality. The defeated Germans signed a treaty that should have prevented them from ever making war again. But with hindsight's clear vision, we can see that the terms of the Treaty of

Versailles created the conditions that bred another war—humiliation, poverty, and a weak government.

In the humiliation of defeat, in economic and political chaos, Germany kept one structure, its military hierarchy, and so rebuilt its military strength. Through the shifting political climate of the 1920s, until Adolf Hitler came to power in 1933, that one institution was constant. In secret defiance of the treaty, an air force was built, weapons were designed, and ships were built that had no purpose except making war. Whatever public reasons the Germans gave, and the Allies accepted, for these activities, only one true reason existed—conquest.

The Allies turned blind eyes to the preparations. The Italian conquest of Ethiopia in 1935 and German and Italian involvement in the Spanish civil war in 1937 showed what air power could do against civilian targets. These two "small" wars also exposed the ruthlessness of the people who controlled Germany and Italy. Poland fell to the Germans in one month—September 1939. In April 1940 the German army, with its Panzer divisions, and the fighters and dive-bombers of the Luftwaffe, began the lightning conquest of continental Europe.

Two months later the German army stood on the Atlantic coast of France, in sight of the last threat to total German control. Twenty-one miles away—visible on a clear day—lay England. The Germans had the entire summer to prepare an invasion fleet and to destroy the primary British defense, the Royal Air Force.

# CHAPTER

# THE
# OPPONENTS

**G**ermany after World War I was ripe for revolutionary movements. Devastating losses of life, in land, in money, and especially in pride had brought great tensions. The economy was at a barter level, for those who were lucky enough to have something to barter.

A weak government, generally supported by the moderate political parties of the center, was threatened on the left by the Bolsheviks—Communists—and on the right by Monarchists and Fascists.

The Bolsheviks were openly revolutionary. Inspired by the success of the revolution that had overthrown the czar in Russia, the Communist movement had spread into western Europe. The middle class feared the Bolsheviks, as did the aristocrats, who also stood to lose all their property should the revolutionaries succeed in establishing a peoples' and workers' state. So those with business or property to protect supported the parties on the political right.

A government that is of the extreme political right is fascist. Fascists support government by one party; state control of privately owned business and industry; and control of the population through censorship, the military, the police, and secret police.

A man was rising in the ranks of a new Fascist political party. The name of the party was the Nationalsozialistische

Deutsche Arbeiterpartei, shortened to Nazi. The man was Adolf Hitler.

Adolf Hitler was the son of an Austrian customs official and a Bavarian woman who worked as a servant. The couple moved often and Adolf never finished high school, but he had been a fairly good student. His ambition was to be an artist, and when he was eighteen he went to Vienna where he twice took and failed the examinations for the Academy of Art. He was very bitter and looked outside himself for the cause of his failure and his poverty.

The lower-middle-class people he associated with had very strong prejudices against Socialists and minority groups, especially Jews. These became the focus of Hitler's bitterness. He became a fanatic in his hatred of Jews and Socialists and in his admiration of the German "race," which he saw as superior to all others.

At the age of twenty-four Hitler went to Munich, and a year later, joined the German army. World War I was beginning, and Hitler's fanaticism made him a brave soldier, twice decorated and wounded. The poison gas both sides used in combat had blinded him temporarily, and he had a long period of darkness in which to think of the wrongs done to Germany and to dream of revenge. When he regained his sight and returned to Munich, he found an atmosphere that mirrored his own feelings of extreme national pride and hatred of Jews. There was a connection imagined by many Germans between Jews and the much-feared Communists.

Hitler became the seventh member of the steering committee for what was to become the Nazi party. He had a real talent for intrigue, for organizing, and above all, for oratory. His own hysterical denunciations of the "enemies" within Germany found ready listeners in the people of what had once been the most feared nation in Europe, a nation that was now stripped of everything but pride.

The Nazi party grew strong on the promise of restoring to Germany its rightful place in commerce, in industry, and most of all, in the eyes of the world as a power to reckon with.

The Nazis found it convenient to preach anti-Semitism, the hatred of the Jews that had flared up during difficult times through the centuries. The Jews had often been blamed, whether the problem was plague, the economy, or military losses. The Nazis found it most useful that their archenemies, the Communists, founded their party on the teachings of a Jew, Karl Marx.

Economic depression gave Hitler his chance. As always in such times, extremists, in this case Communists, fanned unrest in the hope of creating the world revolution that Marx had predicted. But the middle class businessmen feared the Communists and saw in the Nazis the saving of the nation. Hitler's nationalist policies, the old imperial colors of red and black in the Nazis' swastika symbol, and the discipline demonstrated by their party's brown-shirted storm troopers appealed to the German need for pride and order. The necessary support of the army was bought with Nazi promises of equipment and prestige. That soothed some of the pain of the surrender so ignominiously forced on Germany by the Treaty of Versailles.

The Nazis deliberately recruited young people. The appeal of economic prosperity and restored pride, and the predominance of youthful leadership, made this a successful ploy. Hitler, Heinrich Himmler, and Josef Goebbels were all under forty-five when they came to power and sixty percent of the Nazi representatives in the Reichstag were under the age of forty.

In 1932 the Nazis gained more Reichstag seats for a total of 230 and became the largest party. A coalition of the Nazis and the Nationalist party elected Hitler chancellor. Franz von Papen of the Nationalist party and two Nazis, Wilhelm Frick and Hermann Goering, became cabinet members. Von Papen, an aristocrat and ex-army officer, was their link to the army, the aristocracy, and the industrialists. He also had influence with President von Hindenburg, which Hitler, the commoner and former enlisted man, did not.

*German workers salute their*
*new Fuehrer, Adolf Hitler.*

Having risen to the position of chancellor by democratic elections, Hitler then set out to destroy the system that had elected him. As many nonelective posts as possible were filled by Nazis. These included the important positions in the official police force and over forty thousand auxiliary policemen. A secret police department was organized. This was the beginning of the Geheime Staatspolizei—the Gestapo.

Then came the opportunity for the Nazis to destroy their most fervent opponents. A fire was set in the Reichstag, in February 1933, just before the elections. It has been claimed that it was deliberately set by the Nazis, but most historians agree that a mentally retarded Dutch anarchist was the arsonist. In any case, it was a chance that the Nazis would not pass up. They claimed it had been set by their political opponents—Communists, Social Democrats, and others. Before morning 4,000 opponents of the Nazis were arrested.

Influenced by von Papen and by the hysteria that the fire seemed to cause, the eighty-six-year-old President von Hindenburg gave Hitler emergency powers. The constitutional rights to free speech, freedom of the press, and free assembly were suspended.

In this turmoil the elections took place, and although the Nazis got only forty-four percent of the vote, almost one hundred of their Reichstag opponents were hiding or in jail. So it was easy for Hitler's Nazi supporters in the Reichstag to vote him complete power of dictatorship.

On August 2, 1934, President von Hindenburg died of natural causes. Parades that had been scheduled for that day for political reasons became memorial parades. Hitler took the opportunity to have the officers and men swear an oath to him, rather than to their country, an oath that was taken as a religious obligation, later preventing many who took it from opposing his poor military decisions or revolting against him:

I swear by God this sacred oath, that I will render unconditional obedience to Adolf Hitler, the Fuehrer of the German Reich and people, Supreme Commander of the Armed Forces, and will be ready as a brave soldier to lay down my life at any time for this oath.

Meanwhile, in Britain in the early 1930s, there was little thought of another European war. Problems within the empire seemed more important—problems like Moslem-Hindu tension in India, a British colony. There, agitation for independence created instability, and until the rule of India passed from Britain to a native government, British money and British soldiers would be needed to maintain control. It was an expensive proposition, and money was not plentiful. Britain was suffering the same economic depression as the rest of Europe and the United States. Rearmament costs money, money that does not show a clear return unless war occurs. Only one strong voice was raised for rearmament. That voice was Winston Churchill's.

A graduate of the Royal Military College, Sandhurst, Churchill had seen service in India, Egypt, and South Africa. He was elected to Parliament in 1900 and remained a member for most of the next sixty-four years. In 1911 his opposition to pacifism was already obvious. As First Lord of the Admiralty, he strengthened the navy for a war he was sure was coming. He mobilized the fleet weeks before World War I began. During and after that war, his military interests and knowledge made him a logical choice for other positions: minister of munitions and, in 1919, secretary of state for war.

In 1932, while Germany was growing stronger and would soon elect Hitler, a charismatic leader who would focus their national efforts on preparing for war, England had elected a parliament reflecting the pacifist sentiments of the voters. Parliament debated the definitions of "offensive" and "defensive" weapons in order to decide which should not be produced by a peace-loving nation.

The German delegates at the 1932 disarmament confer-

ence in Geneva demanded that the Versailles Treaty restrictions on their rearmament be removed. In Britain there was support for this action. A major newspaper, *The Times* (of London), called it "redress of inequality." Various plans were brought up to equalize the military strength of Germany with that of other nations. These plans called for the Allies to reduce their military production and to destroy their heavier weapons while Germany built up to military equality. However, when this "equalizing" plan was presented at the disarmament conference in 1933, the new German chancellor, Adolf Hitler, did not bother to respond. He withdrew Germany from the conference and from the League of Nations. He had already directed an all-out and public German effort to increase the military preparations that had secretly existed for several years.

In 1933 the students of the Oxford Union passed a resolution "that this house refuses to fight for king and country." Winston Churchill later wrote:

> Little did the foolish boys who passed the resolution dream that they were destined quite soon to conquer or fall in the ensuing war and to prove themselves the finest generation ever to be bred in Britain. Less excuse can be found for their elders who had no chance of self-repudiation in action.

During the years of pacifism, Churchill spoke almost alone in the House of Commons against the policies of appeasement.

*Sir Winston Churchill
warned his countrymen
against the Nazi menace,
but few listened during
the years of pacifism
in the 1930s.*

Repeatedly he pointed out the danger of ignoring the Nazi-led rise of German militarism. In all the ways he could, he supported British defense building.

Among Churchill's opponents was a British pro-German group. The editor of *The Times* favored Germany because he disliked the French. And there were those among the aristocrats who saw Nazi Germany as restoring the German Empire—a sort of good-old-days philosophy. Some people admired the order of the Nazi regime, and many felt guilty for the heavy burdens placed on Germany by the Treaty of Versailles. Also, many politicians preferred to focus attention on the British Empire, and not on European problems. These factors—the pacifist movement, and the very strong hatred of communism shared with the Nazis—kept Parliament from dealing with the growing German power and the shrinking British military capacity.

Churchill continued to speak up in Parliament and to monitor the status of military preparedness in all the countries likely to be involved in a European conflict. In March 1934 he pointed out to the House of Commons the position of Britain in terms of air power—the fifth strongest. Germany, he reminded the Commons, was breaking the Treaty of Versailles, confident that no other country would go to war over its violations.

He went on to predict that within a year and a half Germany would have the capability of attacking Britain. Most people knew that the Germans had an "air sport" pilot-training program that could someday be applied to military use. The Germans also had clandestine agreements with the Soviet Union, their supposed enemy, to train Germans in Russian military planes. And a real German air force did exist. It was illegal and a badly kept secret which was in fact known to a number of people in Britain.

"We take Germany as the ultimate potential enemy, against whom our long-range defense policy must be directed," said Stanley Baldwin in 1933. This was the year

Hitler became chancellor and Germany walked out of the disarmament conference. Baldwin had been and would again be prime minister, and between the two periods in which he held that office, he was a powerful party leader who greatly influenced policy.

During those years from 1924 to 1937, in office and out, his approach to national defense and rearmament was, at best, confusing, and at worst, ineffectual. In 1934 he said, "The bomber will always get through. The only defense is offense." But that same year less was spent on Britain's air defenses than in 1932. When plans for building aircraft were made, they were not carried out. Baldwin's chancellor of the Exchequer (similar to the U.S. secretary of the treasury) was Neville Chamberlain. Part of his job was to advise on spending, and he persistently advised Baldwin to cut back on defense spending. The result was a failure to plan or to carry out the few plans made. Baldwin failed to use his cabinet's advice as had been the tradition for prime ministers. He only took advice that reflected his own feelings, and for that he turned to Neville Chamberlain.

In 1935 the British pacifist movement was at its height. So many British still had faith in the League of Nations that their own sense of self-reliance was undermined. A number of plays and books, well and effectively written, increased the British sense of disillusionment. *Testament of Youth, All Quiet on the Western Front,* and *A Farewell To Arms* grimly described the world war only fifteen years before. Old memories of those terrible times fed the pacifist cause. One hundred thousand men signed a peace pledge:

> I renounce war and never again will I support or sanction another, and I will do all in my power to persuade others to do the same.

Pacifist sentiment, economic difficulties, admiration for the Nazi accomplishments, and apathy prevailed. The plan for military preparation presented to Parliament by the Conservative party was a five-year plan to achieve parity with Germany. But Germany, it was clear, would be strong enough to start a war within eighteen months! Nevertheless, the Labour and Liberal parties actually opposed even the minimal effort of the five-year plan.

Churchill spoke on behalf of his party's plan, even though he thought it inadequate, because it was the only plan to propose any increase in British air power. He said the secret German air force was already two-thirds the strength of the British, and that by the end of 1935 the two nations would be nearly equal. He pointed out that once Germany had the lead it would be hard to catch up. With new factories already operating, Germany could maintain the lead over Britain, which had not even built factories.

A few months later Churchill expanded his prediction to say that by the end of 1937 the German air force would be *twice* as strong as the British. The prime minister, Stanley Baldwin, said that was a great exaggeration, a reassurance that soothed most of the members of Parliament. By March of 1935 Baldwin had to admit that Germany had reached a strength equal to Britain's in air power, and by the end of that year would be fifty percent stronger. But it was not until May that Baldwin admitted that he had misjudged the German intentions and capacity for production. Even then the opponents of a total British commitment to rearmament dragged their feet and insisted that the obligation to oppose Germany had to be shared with other nations.

One positive event that occurred during these years of indecision in Britain was the design of two new aircraft. In November 1935 the prototype of the Hurricane flew, and in March of 1936 the first Spitfire was in the air. This became a British advantage, as their new planes were of later design than the Germans' principal fighter, the Messerschmitt 109. The British lack of quantity was somewhat compensated by quality.

Another vital area of preparation for war in which the Germans were well ahead was manpower. Beginning with the Hitler Youth organization, young people were indoctrinated with nationalist fervor and Nazi loyalty. Again one of the few voices raised in warning was that of Winston Churchill. He had addressed the House of Commons in November of 1933:

> . . . we see that a philosophy of bloodlust is being inculcated into their youth to which no parallel can be found since the days of barbarism. We see all these forces on the move, and we must remember that this is the same mighty Germany which fought all the world and almost beat the world; it is the same mighty Germany which took two and a half lives for every German life taken. No wonder . . . that there is alarm throughout the whole circle of nations which surround Germany.

The Hitler Youth voluntarily went into work battalions that built roads, bridges, and public buildings. In 1935 this duty became compulsory for all German males when they reached the age of twenty. The indoctrination continued, stressing social unity and abolition of class lines. From the work battalions the young men went directly into military service for two years. The army took over the responsibility of educating and unifying the citizens of the Third Reich. Each soldier took an oath of loyalty, not to the nation, but to the Fuehrer.

The establishment of the draft in 1935 (another treaty violation) made the German army, already a force to reckon with, even stronger. Between 1934 and 1940 three million men were drafted. Although the Treaty of Versailles outlawed conscription, as well as the secret air force, nothing was done by the other nations to formally oppose these moves or even protest them.

# CHAPTER

# THE
# REHEARSALS

**A**lthough the Allied nations seemed blind to the Fascist threat, they had many opportunities to confirm the danger and to observe the weapons that would soon be turned against them.

In Italy, Benito Mussolini had led the Italian Fascist party to power and, in fact, had given the movement its name. (The Latin word *fasces* means a bundle of rods which was an emblem of power of a Roman judge.) Mussolini, like Hitler, exploited his nation's feelings of inferiority to inspire his people to prove themselves stronger and superior to the rest of the world. He looked for a "cause" to unite Italians and impress the world. He found it in North Africa.

Italy had an African colony, Somaliland, that bordered on Ethiopia. In 1896 the Italians had been defeated by the Ethiopians and their troops had been killed, captured, and even mutilated by the natives, who often were armed only with spears. In 1935 Mussolini made it a matter of national pride to avenge the loss and to make Ethiopia an Italian colony.

At the League of Nations Assembly in Geneva, the British representative Anthony Eden persuaded the Assembly to invoke sanctions against Italy. This meant member nations would not give financial aid or supplies to Italy and would give their assistance to Ethiopia. Two British battle cruisers— the *Hood* and the *Reknown*—a cruiser squadron, and a destroyer flotilla arrived at Gibraltar. It appeared that Britain was prepared to support the League stand. There was some popular support for this stand, especially among the trade unions, which had seen fascist governments destroy unions in Italy and Germany.

But Prime Minister Baldwin was not prepared to go to war, nor was he truly ready to support the sanctions Britain's own League representative had proposed. The British navy was in the Mediterranean, but it never met the Italian navy in battle. Strategic materials like iron and oil arrived in Italy, and supplies flowed freely from Italy to its army in Ethiopia.

Private manufacturers in member countries, including Britain and France, continued to sell arms to Italy while their governments actually enlarged those exports for Ethiopia. Most of the opposition to Italy was verbal, but the public thought the League was actually doing something.

In his memoirs of World War II, Winston Churchill said the lack of decisive action at this time caused Hitler to think Britain was, and would remain, vacillating and weak. Thus encouraged, Hitler took the steps that led to the war.

The Italian takeover of Ethiopia began in February of 1936. This time the invasion by a highly mechanized European army against native troops with primitive weapons had a foregone conclusion. The Italians horrified the world by using poison gas, and they bombed and strafed both soldiers and civilians. Air power as a weapon of terror was introduced.

This victory encouraged Fascist movements in Poland, Yugoslavia, Hungary, Rumania, and Bulgaria, all of which would eventually join, or be dragged into, the German-Italian alliance that had begun in 1935.

Hitler, meanwhile, was preparing to see how far he could go against the vacillating Allies. His growing military strength—submarines for the navy, conscription for the army, the no-longer-secret air force—was being ignored or accepted by much of Europe, as well as by the United States.

The chance for a united effort and decisive defeat of Fascist expansionism was thrown away when nothing substantial was done to help Ethiopia. The democracies together would still be potentially far stronger, but they were only united in their inability to take a stand. As Churchill said,

> Virtuous motives, trammelled by inertia and timidity, are no match for armed and resolute wickedness. A sincere love of peace is no excuse for muddling hundreds of millions of humble folk into total war.

Eleven million of those people who would soon be at war had, in 1935, answered a "Peace Ballot," an unofficial survey of British opinion on reasons for going to war. It was ambiguously worded and could be claimed as support by both sides of the rearmament-disarmament question. The eleven million British favored the League of Nations and international agreements to reduce armaments. But—and it is a very important "but"—they also agreed that if nonmilitary measures did not restrain an aggressor, military measures should be used. For the next five years, the party in power, the Conservatives, considered only the first half of this response. And German power increased.

On March 7, 1936, Hitler invited the ambassadors of Britain, France, Belgium, and Italy to a meeting in which he proposed a twenty-five-year nonaggression pact. In fact, the proposal was hardly different from the current agreements, the Versailles Treaty (1919) and the Treaty of Locarno (1925): demilitarization of both sides of the Rhine River, limitation of air forces, and nonaggression pacts with Germany's neighbors to the east and west.

On the same day, two hours later, Hitler announced to the Reichstag that Germany was reclaiming the Rhineland. A German army of thirty-five thousand marched into all the major towns, where they were received with joy. The act was presented as "symbolic." The only official objection came from France, which again saw the dreaded Germans on its border.

France turned to Britain, its ally, for assurance of support. Britain urged an appeal to the League of Nations. France was at this time strong enough alone to have driven the Germans out of the Rhineland, but did nothing. The combined force of Britain, France, and the French allies—Czechoslovakia, Yugoslavia, Rumania, and the Baltic states, including Poland—could have permanently stopped Hitler. Hitler himself said to the Austrian chancellor, Kurt von Schuschnigg, "If France had marched then, we would have been forced to withdraw." It was also learned years later that the show of such unity would have destroyed Hitler's credibility with his generals, and he would surely have been removed from office.

The British press maintained belief in Hitler's nonaggression pact. The representative British view of the Rhineland was expressed by Lord Lothian, who said, "After all, they're only going into their own back garden."

Hitler and Mussolini exchanged visits and impressed the world with military reviews to show the growing might of their armies. Their alliance formed the Rome-Berlin Axis. They had a chance to demonstrate their unity of purpose in Spain and again convincingly demonstrated the use of air power as a weapon of terror and destruction of civilian targets.

In 1936 Spain was deeply torn by a struggle that began between the Republicans, representing urban workers—often Communist—and the monarchists, supported by the nobility, much of the army, and the hierarchy of the Catholic Church. Those supporting the old monarchy, the Church, and the army formed a fascist movement called the Falange. The moderates tended to support the Republicans, in a coalition called the Popular Front. In July of 1936 civil war broke out, and each side appealed to nations likely to support its cause.

Italy and Germany came in quickly on the side of the Falangists, who were led by General Francisco Franco. Italy sent bombers and Germany sent transport planes, which were essential for bringing Spanish troops from Moroccan bases. Germany also sent fighters and bombers. Italy sent forty-eight thousand soldiers, who fought poorly and were defeated in a major battle. This was an embarrassment to the Italian government; to regain its prestige, it sent more troops and planes.

Russia supported the Republicans, with planes, tanks, and arms, but because Russia had to send supplies through the Mediterranean where German and Italian warships prowled, Russian aid was somewhat limited. France secretly helped the Republicans and would have helped openly but for internal opposition from nonsocialists as well as opposition from Britain. There the Conservatives, whose party was in power, supported the Spanish Nationalists—the party of the nobles, the landowners—those who seemed most like the British Conservatives.

Britain therefore proposed to France, Germany, Italy, and Russia a policy of nonintervention in the Spanish civil war. Germany and Italy delayed agreeing to it until they knew the Falangists had won. The policy of nonintervention gave Hitler and Mussolini great encouragement to believe the democracies would not resist further aggression in other nations.

Despite the official hands-off position of Allied governments, men from Great Britain, the United States, and France, as well as anti-Fascist refugees from Germany and Italy, came to Spain to fight for the Republican cause. These foreign volunteers formed the International Brigade. Some came to fight against fascism, and some came to fight for socialism or communism.

Ranged against the idealists was the formidable power of the Fascists. The world learned again of that new tactic of war, terror bombing. The Luftwaffe's Condor Legion held what Hitler later described as a rehearsal for the war to come. The most terrible example of the Legion's power in the air came in the bombing of Guernica, a small town in northern Spain. Over twenty-five hundred civilians were killed out of a population of six thousand. The town had no strategic significance.

The Germans bombed many other Republican towns, including Madrid. The Stukas that would later be seen in the blitzkrieg, the "lightning war" in which the Germans overran Europe, were used first in Spain. Overall, the impression remained that air power was *the* weapon of the future and that effective defense against it did not exist.

The bloody Spanish war went on, ferocious as are most civil wars. The Falangists were especially brutal, slaughtering whole populations in towns that had been held by the Republicans. The war continued into 1939, and all this time German power was being demonstrated elsewhere in Europe as well. Following their reoccupation of the Rhineland, the Germans had begun to build their answer to France's Maginot line. This line was a series of fortifications and gun emplacements designed to control the border between Germany and France from Switzerland to Luxembourg. Germany's fortifications, called the Siegfried line, faced the French.

The Spanish civil war and the Siegfried line temporarily faded into the background in Britain as a new crisis arose. In the fall of 1936 King Edward VIII declared his intention to marry the twice-divorced American, Wallis Warfield Simpson. As king, Edward was titular head of the Church of England, which did not sanction divorce. His intended wife would not be officially recognized, nor could any child of that marriage inherit the throne. And most important, if the king married against the disapproval of the cabinet, the cabinet would resign. This could cause a constitutional crisis.

Also, while the British monarch has little legal power, he has great influence. This situation could divide the people, and so the problem was considered critical. Edward decided, with support from Baldwin and advice from

Churchill, that he would abdicate the throne to his brother, who was crowned George VI. It was Baldwin's last important act as prime minister to present this act to the British people without disturbing that necessary morale factor, the influence of the monarch.

Baldwin's retirement followed soon after. Unfortunately, he had groomed to succeed him his Chancellor of the Exchequer, that noted opponent of arms expenditures and proponent of diplomatic solutions, Neville Chamberlain.

Chamberlain had been a successful Lord Mayor of Birmingham, doing much to improve the living conditions of his constituents. He was a very able minister of health in Baldwin's first term as prime minister. No one doubted his administrative abilities in these offices, but his temperament and beliefs proved totally unsuited to the office of prime minister in the critical years of 1937 to 1940.

Harold Wilson, who served as prime minister in 1964–1970 and 1974–1976, described Chamberlain as "totally opinionated, totally certain he was right." He would not take the advice of his cabinet. Indeed, the only person he listened to was one close friend, Horace Wilson, who had been an industrial mediator and was convinced the tactics that brought settlements between management and labor would also settle international disputes. Wilson was even less qualified to make national decisions than the former Lord Mayor of Birmingham. Wilson was a yes-man and so got on well with Chamberlain. Anyone who disagreed with Chamberlain found himself labeled as disloyal by both the prime minister and the newspapers that supported him.

The three years Chamberlain was in office, the main issues were rearmament and appeasement. The two were bound together, for Chamberlain felt the threat of conquest by Germany and its ally Italy could be removed by making concessions. His main theme was that England should not commit any act that Hitler or Mussolini could interpret as warlike. That included any increase in military strength.

Meanwhile, Germany's next goal was to annex Austria,

which had the same language and a similar culture. Germany had long pressed for the two nations to be joined. Now the Austrian Nazi party was under German control, and through open political maneuvers and secret undermining of the democratic system, the Nazis were gaining power. In February 1938 the Austrian government tried to suppress Nazi activity and, in great indignation, Hitler protested and moved German military units near the Austrian border. Fearing an invasion, the Austrian chancellor agreed to allow some Nazi representation in the government. It soon became obvious that the Nazis would take over, so the chancellor called a plebiscite for March 13 in which the people could vote on whether they wanted to be independent of Germany.

Hitler demanded postponement of the plebiscite, and claiming that Austrian authorities could not maintain order, sent his troops into Austria. On March 14, 1938, German troops marched into Vienna. Hitler returned to that city where he had been a poor youth, and he returned in triumph as the leader of the now-combined nations. Churchill, with his usual foresight, said, "Austria has been laid in thrall, and we do not know whether Czechoslovakia will not suffer a similar attack."

Hitler's next move did come against Czechoslovakia. The Treaty of Versailles had given the Sudetenland to Czechoslovakia, but many Germans, including some who continued to live in the Sudeten area, felt that it should be German. Hitler claimed that the German people had the need for, and the right to, that space for their expanding population. The Czechoslovakian government, in addition to having a natural resistance to that idea, also knew the loss of that area would mean it could no longer remain independent of German influence. The Czech fortifications in the Sudeten were their basic defense against German aggression. Giving it up would leave them open to invasion. The British had remained on the sidelines during the Italian campaign in Ethiopia, the Spanish civil war, and the German takeover of Austria. But German threats against Czechoslovakia were going to bring in treaty obligations that the French and Russians had with Czechoslovakia. If they were forced to go to war with Hitler, the British, who had treaty obligations with the French, would be drawn in as well.

In Britain, pacifist sentiment still ran high, and no one was more anxious to avoid war than the current prime minister, Neville Chamberlain. Chamberlain hated war, and he hated to spend national resources on preparing for a war that he believed could be avoided. Chamberlain himself said, in a private letter of March 20, 1938,

> You have only to look at the map to see that nothing that France or we could do could possibly save Czechoslovakia from being overrun by the Germans, if they wanted to do it . . . I have, therefore, abandoned any idea of giving guarantee to Czechoslovakia, or to the French in connection with her obligations to that country.

He was convinced that diplomacy could successfuly solve most problems, and that Hitler would be susceptible to reason—British reason.

Hitler's reasoning, however, was that German expansion was necessary to insure enough living space, enough access to cropland and raw materials, more easily defended frontiers, and more manpower for the German war industry. Czechoslovakian arms factories were making some of the best weapons in the world—a very desirable objective for the Nazis.

A Nazi party had been formed in Czechoslovakia, and its members constantly agitated for cession of the Sudeten to Germany, for changes in Czech foreign policy that would be favorable to Germany, and for breaking ties with the Russians. The Nazis tried to disrupt political meetings and had frequent clashes with the Czech police. All this was similar to the Nazi campaigns in Austria.

France, meanwhile, as an ally of Czechoslovakia, was trying to persuade Britain to stand firm to prevent a German takeover. The French premier Daladier said that peace would be preserved if Britain and France stood firm. The Russians offered assistance if the two nations committed themselves to defend Czechoslovakia. The Russian offer was ignored, an act that was to haunt the British later. Chamberlain would not threaten war if he were not willing to take Britain to war—and he was firmly against that. He was convinced Hitler's threats were bluff.

The British press was still favoring a course of appeasement. On September 7, 1938, a lead article in *The Times* suggested the Czech government should consider, for the sake of peace with Germany, ceding to Germany the areas of Czechoslovakia with large German populations. Although the British government claimed that was not an expression of official sentiments, French public opinion reflected the fear that it was just that. The French greatly feared facing Germany without British support.

Pressure for settlement of the Sudeten question increased. The Germans threatened and the Czech Nazis agitated. While the situation was becoming ominous in the opinion of the British and French, they did not make any strong moves to counteract it. Seeing their strongest supporters wavering, the Czechs agreed to mediation.

While the mediation efforts were in progress, Hitler was stirring up German sentiment for the "poor" Sudeten Germans, who, he claimed, were living under oppression. The Czech Nazis started riots, and in the pretense of defending the Sudeten Germans, Germany seemed prepared to go to war. Chamberlain asked Hitler to discuss the problem with him personally, and on Hitler's agreement, flew to Germany where he met Hitler at Berchtesgaden.

Chamberlain had a hard time pinning Hitler down on what terms would be acceptable to solve the Czech problem. Eventually they agreed that Czechoslovakia should give independence to regions in which more than fifty percent of the inhabitants were German. Chamberlain returned to London and discussed the matter with the French premier and foreign secretary. They presented the Czechs with the terms and also with the warning that the Germans would attack if the terms were not met. The Czechs reluctantly conceded. When informed of this development on Chamberlain's second visit, Hitler said the terms had changed. Czechoslovakia must pull out of the regions specified, and the Germans would occupy them. When that was accomplished, an international commission could settle the minor details. Chamberlain was trying to decide how to respond to these new demands when the Czech Nazis formally asked Germany to help them to "protect" themselves. They were given weapons by the Germans and began taking over some Sudeten towns. Chamberlain urged Hitler to have another conference, and Hitler agreed to have one in Munich with representatives from Britain, France, and Italy. No one seemed to care that the Czechs were not invited to the conference. The representatives of the four nations at the conference agreed to give Hitler what he wanted. The Sudetenland was turned over to Germany on September 30, 1938. Chamberlain was convinced that the sacrifice of Czechoslovakia had finally satisfied the Germans' demands for new territory. Surely they would now have no need or desire to threaten the peace of Europe.

Ecstatic crowds greeted Chamberlain on his return to Britain. He was hailed as a great peacemaker, and the newspapers and the general public expressed a great sense of relief that war had been averted. But things did not go so smoothly in the House of Commons.

There, Winston Churchill, seeing the true meaning of appeasement, had already said, a week before the final Munich meeting,

The partition of Czechoslovakia under pressure from England and France amounts to the complete surrender of the Western Democracies to the Nazi threat of force. Such a collapse will bring peace or security

Neville Chamberlain, holding aloft
the Munich agreement, is greeted by
crowds who applaud his promise that
there would be no war.

neither to England nor to France. On the contrary, it will place these two nations in an ever weaker and more dangerous situation. The mere neutralisation of Czechoslovakia means the liberation of twenty-five German divisions, which will threaten the Western Front; in addition to which it will open up for the triumphant Nazis the road to the Black Sea. It is not Czechoslovakia alone which is menaced, but also the freedom and the democracy of all nations. The belief that security can be obtained by throwing a small state to the wolves is a fatal delusion. The war potential of Germany will increase in a short time more rapidly than it will be possible for France and Great Britain to complete the measures necessary for their defense.

Churchill was of Chamberlain's own party, the Conservatives, as was Duff Cooper, First Lord of the Admiralty, who resigned that post because he disagreed so strongly with the Munich settlement. Clement Attlee of the Labour party said,

We have felt we are in the midst of a tragedy. We have felt humiliation. This has not been a victory for reason and humanity. It has been a victory for brute force.

Sir Archibald Sinclair, the Liberal leader, gave the warning that

a policy which imposes injustice on a small and weak nation and tyranny on free men and women can never be the foundation of lasting peace.

But Chamberlain had the support of the rank-and-file Conservatives and the consolation of receiving piles of favorable mail. As a later prime minister, Harold Wilson, said, "It is when a prime minister evaluates his postbag as an offset to Parliament that democracy is in danger."

Following Munich, pleas to increase aircraft production were met with the Chamberlain response that such an increase would be seen as a sign that Britain was abandoning the Munich agreement. Also he felt that since Germany was unlikely to violate Belgian neutrality and the French Maginot line completed the containment of Germany on its western border, increases in British aircraft production were unnecessary.

But quite a different point of view was Hitler's. He was reported as saying

> If I were Chamberlain, I would not delay for a minute to prepare my country for the most drastic total war. . . . If the English have not got universal conscription by the spring of 1939 they may consider their world empire lost. It is astounding how easy the democracies make it for us to reach our goal.

This viewpoint was not lost on many British, in spite of Chamberlain's mail and the backing of many Conservatives in Parliament. Churchill wrote of the passions that raged in Britain for and against the Munich agreement:

> Men and women, long bound together by party ties, social amenities and family connections glared upon one another in scorn and anger.

There was a three-day debate in Parliament, preceded by the resignation speech of Duff Cooper. Cooper reviewed the list of Hitler's actions: the broken treaties (Versailles and Locarno); his promise that he had no further territorial claims in Europe, followed by the invasion of Austria; and the assurance he would not interfere in Czechoslovakia, followed by the takeover of half that country. Yet, Cooper pointed out, Chamberlain still felt he could rely on Hitler's good faith.

Cooper also said if Britain had gone to war over Czechoslovakia, it would have been to prevent one country, Germany, from dominating Europe by "brutal force." That "brutal force" was almost immediately demonstrated in German-occupied Czechoslovakia, where anti-Nazis were arrested, tortured, and executed by the Gestapo. In November 1938 a pogrom against the Jews began. Thousands of Jews were murdered, Jewish shops and synagogues were burned, the Jewish community had to pay eighty million pounds to repair the damages their enemies had done, and then Jews were excluded from all economic activity. Cooper concluded that against German domination Britain "must ever be prepared to fight, for on the day we are not prepared to fight for it, we forfeit our Empire, our liberties and our independence."

# CHAPTER

# THE
# BEGINNING

**P**eace in our time" was a very brief comfort to the British. Relief that war had been averted mingled with fear that the lull was only temporary and with shame that the democracy of Czechoslovakia had been sacrificed. That fear spurred British rearmament efforts. But the Germans were still producing at a faster rate. The British brought forty-seven squadrons of Hurricanes and Spitfires (507 aircraft) on the line by the summer of 1940—their primary and most vital improvement. But the growth in German manufacture of war materials overall far outstripped the British and the French because the Germans had been working openly toward full production since 1936—nearly three critical years longer than the Allies.

Munitions production on a nationwide scale, according to Churchill, would take four years. Designing weapons, building factories, creating machinery, and training workers to reach full production is a long task. The Germans had already invested heavily. German expenditures on this task in 1938 and 1939 were five times the British.

Time was not the only loss for the British. Other losses were the twenty-one Czech army divisions no longer available to defend against Germany and the Czech fortifications that, prior to the Munich agreement, had required thirty German divisions to guard against Czech support of any Allied cause. And as ominous as the loss of Czech manpower was the German takeover of Czech armament factories. Skoda Works alone produced nearly enough weapons to equal the entire British production. Czech tanks and guns were considered among the world's best.

And less easily measured, but of great importance, was German morale. Success had given the Germans confidence and increased their already warlike attitude. The French and British had to deal with the fact that on every diplomatic front they had retreated. The French, obligated by treaty to support Czechoslovakia, had a great sense of honor lost.

Hitler hoped to discourage the British from maximum preparation for war. He accused Churchill, and others who favored the swiftest possible rearmament, of being warmongers and said that their actions would start a war. He also seemed to be making efforts to convince the French that he posed no threat to them. Hitler had his eye out for other victims. He was looking to the east, at what remained of Czechoslovakia, at Lithuania, and at Poland.

Germany accomplished Czechoslovakia's final dissolution by open threat. German troops crossed the border, and to avoid useless slaughter, the Czech president signed away the independence of his country. Under threat the Lithuanians gave up their Baltic port of Memel, which had a large German population. By the end of March 1939, the question was not *if* Hitler would attack someone else, but *whom* he would attack. Would he look east to Poland and Russia or west to France, the Low Countries, and Britain?

In Britain public opinion was finally changing. Pacifism evaporated in the face of Hitler's open aggression in the final takeover of Czechoslovakia. The Sudeten giveaway had been acceptable to some because they thought the large German population there preferred unity with Germany. But the total takeover of the rest of the country was beyond such explanation. It was aggression: Hitler had blatantly broken his promises not to make any more territorial demands in Europe, not to extend his rule to the rest of Czechoslovakia, and not to settle disputes by force. It became understood, finally, that Hitler's purpose was the conquest of Europe.

Chamberlain was heavily criticized for agreeing to the giveaway of Czechoslovakia. To show that his government was not prepared to tolerate any more, he gave guarantees that Britain would support Poland and Russia—the next nations likely to be threatened by Hitler. France also promised its support in a mutual assistance pact that Denmark, the Netherlands, and Switzerland also joined. But Chamberlain continued to believe that Hitler would see that he could not win a war against the British navy and the French army.

The United States had, at that time, a neutrality law that, if followed, would prevent American aid to Europe. Attempts were made to modify the law to allow the United States to supply materials to Britain, but the law remained intact. The German diplomats reported to Hitler that the United States would rescind the law and intervene if there were danger of a British defeat. But they also said that the American military position was weak, and that no help could be given for at least six months once it was decided to help Britain. This was also a common opinion in Britain, and many thought that the most powerful ally for Britain to seek would be Russia.

The Russians and the Germans seemed natural enemies. Politically they were opposites—at least in theory. Fascism was a government from the top down; the dictator, or a small group, controlled all means of production and could direct all its citizens' efforts toward any purpose. Communism was, according to its claims, government from the bottom up; the people owned everything. The real source of their enmity, however, was that both the Fascists and the Communists sought control of Europe, the Fascists by conquest and the Communists by revolution. They had fought each other in the streets of many European cities. Large German populations lived in the areas of Russia nearest the expanding German empire, and Russia had interests in its former ally, Czechoslovakia, and in Poland.

While debate went on in Britain and France about the wisdom of a British–Russian alliance, Hitler and the Russian dictator Stalin were secretly making their own arrangements. On August 22, 1939, the German government announced it would sign a nonaggression pact with the Soviet Union. For this guarantee that he would not have to defend his eastern borders against Russia, Hitler had to promise that the Baltic countries of Finland, Lithuania, Latvia, and Estonia, and parts of Poland and Rumania, would be left to the Soviets. This shocked Britain and France, which had expected the Russians to keep Hitler threatened on his eastern borders.

On September 1, 1939, Germany invaded Poland. On September 3 Great Britain and France declared war on Germany. By the end of September, Poland was defeated. The Polish cavalry and obsolete fighters could not stand up to panzer divisions and the Luftwaffe. As the victorious Germans swept through Poland, the SS followed close behind, murdering most of the aristocrats, government officials, doctors, lawyers, teachers, and Jews. They intended that no one would be left except laborers. There would be no leaders to organize a resistance.

British and French support of Poland did not mean they immediately rushed into battle, even though the French had agreed to attack within two weeks of Poland's being attacked. Had they done so, they would have found Germany's western border only weakly defended. But France needed time to mobilize its forces, and a long lull occurred, which the British called the "Phony War." This lasted until the following spring, when, on April 9, 1940, Hitler launched his next invasion.

The invasion of Poland shook the confidence of Parliament in Chamberlain, but not enough to force his resignation. He bowed to pressure to bring into his cabinet men with more military knowledge. The choice of Winston Churchill to be First Lord of the Admiralty—the post he had held in

World War I—was popular. In fact, his appointment was announced to all the ships and naval bases with the wire, "Winston is back." No more needed to be said. They felt they were at last in good hands.

The British Expeditionary Force (BEF), almost the entire professional army based in Britain, moved to France immediately upon the declaration of war. The BEF moved, along with French units, into positions along the Belgian border and eastward to connect with the French Maginot line. There they sat during the "Phony War."

Belgium, for its part, remained determined to be neutral. A treaty between Belgium, France, and Britain provided only that Belgium could, if it wished, invite the others to give assistance. The Allies could not go in without an invitation, and neutral Belgium was not requesting assistance. The Germans had an advantage here; the Allies could not attack the Ruhr, the German industrial area, because they would have to go through Belgium to get to it. As a neutral country, Belgium actually, although unintentionally, gave the advantage to the Germans, who would not be finicky about neutrality.

But this advantage was not so obvious when the British and French set up their defenses. France's Maginot line seemed impregnable. Miles of underground fortifications were connected by subway. Huge guns controlled from underground bunkers could destroy anything, it seemed, that tried to break through. This network stretched along the French-German border to Belgium. The Belgian border from Germany to the sea was defended by the BEF and units of the French army. The French army was large, and had highly respected commanders, and modern armaments. It was thought to be the most powerful army in the world. The Germans had a fortified line of their own, the Siegfried line, to protect the weakest area of their side of the border. It seemed to the high commands of both sides that an army invading in either direction faced very high risks.

But Hitler had proven that the Allies were not strong-willed when he invaded Austria, Czechoslovakia, and

Poland. He believed that the French army was weak and that the British did not have the will to fight. He had become so powerful that he could override all objections by his generals. The only question was which way the attack should be made, and on this, both the German and the British high commands came to the same conclusion. The attack would come through the Netherlands and Belgium. The BEF fortified its line and waited.

The British navy did not have to wait; the Germans immediately began their U-boat (submarine) campaign. On the night of September 3, 1939, the British passenger liner *Athenia* was torpedoed and sank, with a loss of 112, including 28 Americans. Two days later the Germans sank three more British ships. The British estimated the German U-boats' active strength at sixty, with another forty expected to be at sea by 1940. They armed all merchant ships with antisubmarine guns, and the navy set up a convoy system so the ships could go in protected groups.

Two weeks later the Germans sank the aircraft carrier *Courageous.* On October 14 a U-boat entered Scapa Flow, the British equivalent of Pearl Harbor, and sank the battleship *Royal Oak,* with 786 men. U-boat harassment of British merchant shipping and naval ships continued. The Germans also dropped magnetic mines from airplanes into the approaches to British harbors. These sank a number of ships before the British designed a means to demagnetize the ships.

The Germans avoided starting anything on their western front, the French and Belgian borders. The main military activity took place to the north. The Russians, going for their rewards for the alliance with Germany, invaded Finland in November of 1939. Although Finland is a small country, the Finns held out against the Russian giant until March 1940, when they finally submitted to the Russians' demands for frontier revisions.

On April 9, 1940, the Germans established themselves in Scandinavia. They overran tiny Denmark and attacked Norway. The German combination of naval and air forces and paratroops overwhelmed the Norwegians. British and French efforts to help were poorly planned and poorly supplied. One positive result of the Allies' defense of Norway was that, while the British navy did have serious losses, it ruined the German surface navy. German sea power, aside from the U-boats, had never compared in numbers to the British, and the Germans would not be able to replace the losses from the Norwegian battles in time to effectively use their surface navy in the Battle of Britain.

In another good result of the Norwegian fiasco, Prime Minister Neville Chamberlain lost the confidence of Parliament. He resigned on May 10 and the Conservative, Liberal, and Labour parties combined to elect the new prime minister, Winston Churchill. As he took office, German paratroops were taking Holland by surprise. Rotterdam was being bombed and nearly destroyed, and German tanks were rolling into Belgium. The Germans moved with incredible speed over the flat farmlands of the Low Countries which, like Poland, had no effective defense against these superbly equipped and trained soldiers.

The French army was undersupplied with antitank and antiaircraft guns and was short of transport to move its troops to the battle zone. The best-equipped French forces were deployed along the Maginot line and were out of the main area of German attack. Responsible for defending the most critical area was the French Ninth Army—mostly middle-aged reservists, recently called up and poorly trained, who

*The industrial city of Rotterdam, Holland, suffered great destruction when Hitler's Wehrmacht swept through the Low Countries.*

had to march seventy-five miles on foot to get to the scene of battle. Weapons and supplies often went by horse-drawn transport in the French army.

The British Expeditionary Force was motorized, but the vehicles were in bad repair. The force had no tanks. Antitank guns were in short supply, as were antiaircraft guns. The BEF's main advantage was that almost the entire force was made up of professional career soldiers. Unfortunately, they were also the main part of the British military organization. If these men were lost, it would be a crippling blow to the British ability to withstand invasion.

The French commanders had control of the British force in that area. In a battle that would move so quickly that flexibility would be an absolute requirement, the French army had a rigid chain of command, which did not allow for battlefield initiative. Another limit to quick response was a poor communications system. The French commander did not have a radio at his headquarters, so communications to the battlefront took as long as forty-eight hours—this against an invading army that had moved as much as thirty miles a day in Poland!

On May 10, 1940, the German army invaded the Netherlands and Belgium. By May 25 the British Expeditionary Force, part of the French First Army, and the Belgian army were reduced to defending the evacuation area around Dunkirk. By June 4 all possible evacuations had been made. The Germans commanded the coast. On June 14 the Germans entered Paris. The Battle of France was over.

Hitler had mastered the Continent. Opposing him alone was the island nation that had not been invaded for nearly nine hundred years. With an air force considerably smaller than the Luftwaffe, they should be vulnerable. If Britain could be successfully invaded, the island would be a pawn. Its people could be held hostage for the surrender of the mighty British fleet. No one recognized this more clearly than Winston Churchill. On June 18, 1940, he addressed Parliament:

The Battle of Britain is about to begin. On this battle depends the survival of Christian civilisation. Upon it depends the survival of our own British life, and the continuity of our institutions and our Empire. The whole fury and might of the enemy must very soon be turned on us. Hitler knows that he will have to break us in this island or lose the war . . . Let us therefore brace ourselves to our duties, and so bear ourselves that, if the British Empire and its common-wealth last for a thousand years, men will say, "This was their finest hour."

# CHAPTER IV

# THE
# DEFENSES

**B**efore World War II the nature of air warfare was largely unknown. Even with new weapons, the armies and navies of the 1940s could still build on the experience of earlier wars. But the air battles of World War I took place between individual pilots. The imagination could no more leap from those experiences to the Battle of Britain—the only major battle ever fought entirely in the air—than it could visualize the Battle of Gettysburg with knowledge only of single combat. No one could predict with assurance what would be the best weapons, the best defenses, the best training. Both sides made many errors as they tried to plan for the coming conflict.

A generally believed theory held that bombers would be the deciding factor. The bomber could destroy enemy defenses and industry, and seemed virtually unstoppable. During the years between the wars, bombers had been used against civilian targets by the Germans in Spain and by the Italians in Ethiopia. There was no doubt that the immediate result had been to terrorize the victims. In fact, that had been the only result, other than the destruction of strategically unimportant buildings. That terror had not been enough to cause the victims to surrender. But in Britain, France, and Germany during the thirties it was accepted that defense against bombers must be impossible, since there was no way to predict their course or target. Therefore it seemed necessary to have more bombers than any potential enemy had.

But there was another way of looking at the problem, and in 1937 the new British minister for the Co-ordination of Defence, Sir Thomas Inskip, had come to another conclusion. He decided that the German expectations of a conflict with Britain were that it would be a short war that would be won by massive bomber attacks. These would destroy morale and bring Britain to the point of making peace on Germany's terms.

Inskip knew that the British could not match German bomber strength at that time and were falling farther behind. He felt that what the British needed most of all was time. They could survive bombing and, with their powerful navy, could survive submarine blockade. Eventually allies would join Britain, and in a long war they would prevail. So what the British must do was to prevent the Germans from forcing them to terms. Britain needed a defense against the bombers. Inskip had some strong cards in his hand. Fighting near their own bases, the British could use their fuel in actual combat rather than in getting to the front. And they had their new system of radar and ground observers.

In 1935 Robert Watson-Watt, a radio expert at Britain's National Physical Laboratories, had mentioned, almost as an afterthought, in a report that there were promising developments in radio detection, a method of locating an object by the radio waves reflected off of it. Air Marshal Hugh Dowding asked for a demonstration, which was very successful. Long-range detection was clearly possible. Furthermore, radar could be used to aim antiaircraft guns. Dowding pressed for further development of the radar—a weapon in what Churchill called "the Wizard's War" because of the many inventions, particularly electronic, that strengthened defenses and increased the power and accuracy of the weapons.

A unique collection of scientists and military men gathered at Bawdsey, a manor near the sea, to develop a functional radar system. It was an ideal atmosphere for the exchange

# THE BATTLE OF BRITAIN

Range of Low-Level Radar

Range of High-Level Radar

Glasgow

Northumberland

Newcastle

FIGHTER
COMMAND
GROUP 13

GREAT BRITAIN

North
Sea

Liverpool

FIGHTER
COMMAND
GROUP 12

Nottingham

Birmingham    Coventry

Norwich

Ipswich

Bawdsey

Swansea

Cardiff

FIGHTER
COMMAND
GROUP 11

Northolt

London

Manston

Croydon    Biggin

Kenley    Hill

Canterbury    Calais

BELGIUM

Bristol

FIGHTER
COMMAND
GROUP 10

Southampton

Tangmere

Hawkinge

Lympne    Wissant

Dunkirk

LUFTFLOTTE 2

Exeter

Portsmouth

St. Omer

Lille

Plymouth

Portland

ENGLISH CHANNEL

Montreuil

Abbeville

Cherbourg

Le Havre

Amiens

Caen

LUFTFLOTTE 3

FRANCE

🗲 Target

▲ RAF Base

□ Sector Station

★ Group Headquarters

of ideas, for it was informal enough for low- and high-ranking people to communicate with each other. The scientists could try out their theories in the situations in which they would be used, and then get feedback directly from the military men who understood the practical aspects. The men at Bawdsey were, above all, practical. They knew there was no time to try for perfection, only workable results.

The device they designed was eventually constructed in a continuous chain of stations around the entire north, south, and east coasts of England and near several seaports on the less vulnerable west coast. Each "Chain Home" station had two sets of huge towers, one set for transmitters and the other for receivers. A signal sent out would either find an object and bounce back or would encounter nothing and not be heard again. The outgoing signal—the "blip"—would appear for a moment on the radar screen. If it was returned, another blip appeared, and the time interval between the two told the operator how far away the aircraft was. Friendly aircraft carried a device called IFF (Identification Friend or Foe), which returned a far stronger signal, alerting the operator that it was a friend.

There were two types of stations: Chain Home stations could detect aircraft as high as twenty thousand feet, and Chain Home Low sets detected low-flying aircraft down to sea level. Since both kinds of radar faced the sea, Fighter Command needed another method to plot aircraft position past the coastline. A civilian Observer Corps used binoculars, aircraft recognition manuals, and altitude-sighting devices to track airplanes reported by incoming radar. These volunteers often had to identify aircraft only by sound, as they flew above the cloud cover.

Distance and altitude were the crucial pieces of information. Operators could calculate the direction in which the incoming enemy planes were flying. By drawing a line from each of two stations to the point where both detected the same aircraft or group of aircraft, they could show the aircraft's exact location at the intersection of the two lines. A series of these intersecting signals would show the course of the plane.

Such information was obviously of crucial importance. But what was unique was the way in which it was used. All the reports of the stations went to the Filter Room at Bawdsey. Here operators plotted the intersecting signals. Since they could compare a number of reports, accuracy was improved. The filtered reports were plotted on a large map table. Enemy aircraft were indicated by red counters and friendly ones by black counters. An arrow showed the direction of the aircraft. Every five minutes the arrow color was changed if new information was received. This way it would be noticed within five minutes if a report had been omitted or lost, indicating the possibility that some friend or enemy had escaped detection or been shot down. WAAFs (Women's Auxiliary Air Force) with earphones, through which they were instructed on the movements of the aircraft, stood around the table and moved the counters in accordance with their telephoned instructions. From a balcony officers watched the whole map and passed on the information to operations rooms at the different levels of command—Sector, Group, and Fighter Command headquarters. Each operations room had an identical map, and thereby a constant stream of accurate and consistent information. A board with colored lights showed each fighter squadron and its state of readiness— whether it could take off in thirty minutes, five minutes, or two minutes or was already in the air.

By using radar and observers in a network of identical maps and extensive communication, the RAF detected both enemy and friendly aircraft before they arrived. The second half of their system covered interception. Each British fighter sent out an automatic signal that the direction-finding station in its sector picked up. These signals appeared on the map, so the Sector Controller could see at a glance where his planes and the enemy's were and direct the interception.

*The RAF plotting room at Fighter
Command headquarters*

The system as a whole, then, worked in the following manner. Incoming aircraft appeared on the radar screens at the Chain Home and Chain Home Low stations. Here they estimated the position, altitude, and number of enemy planes. This information went to the Filter Room at Fighter Command Headquarters, where it was plotted on the map table and identified as friend or enemy or unknown. Fighter Command Operations, Group Operations, and Sector Operations of those sectors involved were notified. In Command Operations they decided whether to sound air-raid alarms and to order any civilian radio stations to shut down, so the enemy planes could not home in on the signals. Group Operations decided which sector would respond and how many fighters to launch. It also decided which antiaircraft guns to use and warned the RAF squadrons clear of that danger. Sector Control had direct supervision of fighter-squadron movements. It gave the orders to put squadrons at thirty-, five-, or two-minute readiness or to launch them. One controller would direct one or two squadrons. The pilots' only knowledge of the enemy's location came from the controller, until visual contact could be made.

There was another important information source for the British. Their intelligence operations had acquired an electrically operated coding machine built in Germany under the name Enigma. The German High Command and Hitler used these machines to communicate with their various military staffs and commanders. The signals could be received by the British and could, by complex mathematics, be decoded. The British were able to acquire a great deal of information about German plans. In the Battle of Britain they often knew the areas that the Luftwaffe would attack and from which direction the attack would come. This intelligence operation, codenamed Ultra, was, along with radar, a major contribution to the British success in the Battle and to Allied successes later in the war.

The British held the "home-field" advantage, which was crucial to their detect-and-intercept defense, since they would know where the enemy was before the enemy knew where the British fighters were. Of course, British airfields were vulnerable to enemy attack, and serious losses occurred there in planes, men, and functioning ability, but this same closeness meant that the English pilots could, and did, fly several sorties in the days of heaviest fighting. The Germans had to return to their bases in France when their fuel was low, which meant that one plane and one pilot equaled one sortie per day. Also, a British pilot who bailed out over land might actually be back in the air and fighting again the same day. The German who bailed out would be a prisoner if he were over England, or had a good chance of drowning or of being picked up by the British if he were in the Channel.

# CHAPTER

# THE
# WEAPONS

**I**n the Battle, the British used two fighters—the Hawker Hurricane and the Supermarine Spitfire. The Hurricane was closer to the old biplanes in construction. Indeed, its designer, Sydney Camm, had evolved its design from the Hawker Fury biplane and the Fury monoplane. The Hurricane had a wire-braced metal-tube framework surrounded with a wood frame, to form the shape, and fabric to cover the wood. The early models had wooden and fabric wings as well, although metal ones were designed before the plane was in full-scale production. While this construction sounds flimsy, the Hurricanes did, in fact, resist damage by exploding shells better than the all-metal aircraft did. And more mechanics had trained in repairing the wood and fabric construction than the metal one.

The Supermarine Spitfire, designed by Reginald Mitchell, evolved from a racing seaplane, the Supermarine S.6B. But several points were of totally new design. It looked like a racing plane—built for speed rather than strength. But the plane was very strong, and the strength was not paid for with added weight but with superior design. The main spar of the wing, for example, was wooden, but it was layered, as a leaf spring in a car is layered, providing greater strength near the root, where there could be more layers, and less bulk farther out, where strength was not so important. The wing

*Pilots of the RAF 87th Squadron rush
to their Hurricane fighter planes to
counter a German attack.*

was capped by a hollow tip. Heavy metal plated the leading edge of the wing, increasing the strength, and lighter metal covered the wing aft of the spar. The shape of the wing was elliptical, curved at the leading and trailing edges, a self-strengthening design. The wide wings distributed the wing load so each part took less stress, and their thinness offered less wind resistance. The combination was a beautiful design, one that was more appreciated in later days when airplanes were going at even higher speeds.

And this wonderful wing still held four machine guns. In armament the Hurricane and the Spitfire were equal. They could fire continuous rounds of three hundred bullets, approximately twelve hundred rounds per minute with each gun.

Both the Hurricane and the Spitfire used the Rolls-Royce Merlin engine. It was made of strong, but light, metal alloys and with supercharger produced 1,175 horsepower. The German designer Willy Messerschmitt did not have such an efficient engine to use in the planes he designed for the Luftwaffe. The most powerful engine produced in Germany— 1,070 horsepower—came from a large, heavy engine built by Daimler-Benz. So his Me 109 needed the smallest, lightest airframe that could possibly carry it. This light construction did not withstand stress as well as its sturdier British counterpart. He mounted two machine guns over the engine and one gun in each wing—a twenty-millimeter cannon. The cannon fired shells that exploded on impact, increasing the possible damage. But the inclusion of wing-mounted guns in the thin wings increased problems of stress already inherent in the design. Later models of the Me 109 had no wing-mounted armament.

Other differences between the fighters of the opposing forces were in armor and maneuverability. Behind the pilot's seat the British plane had armor plate, which the Germans envied, and with good reason. It saved a number of lives. The German fighter had a tighter turning radius, an important advantage in a dogfight, but pilots did not often use it, since the wings were not strong enough to withstand the forces created in such tight turns. At the beginning of the Battle, the Germans had constant-speed propellers, which increased the 109's service ceiling (maximum altitude for normal flying). The British began the Battle with fixed-pitch and two-position propellers. But by August 15 all the Hurricanes and Spitfires had been fitted with the constant-speed props.

The Spitfire and the Me 109 had similar flying characteristics. But the Spitfire's bubble hood provided better visibility. The German plane had thicker framework in the canopy, and the rear view was blocked by the fuselage. However, the Spitfire did not recover as well from spins. Spitfires with their stronger airframes seemed less likely to break up in the air from overstressing. The Messerschmitt's weaker wings and tail could withstand less damage and less stress from aerial maneuvers.

At the beginning of the Battle the Germans had a far greater number of aircraft—over eight hundred fighters and one thousand bombers. The British had some seven hundred fighters. But the British produced five hundred Hurricanes and Spitfires per month as compared to one hundred forty Me 109s and ninety Me 110s that the Germans put out monthly. The British began with thirteen hundred pilots and approximately fifty per week coming out of training. The Germans had a total of ten thousand pilots in 1939, but, of course, a far smaller number had actual operational experience. Overall, though they did have more experienced pilots than the British, that advantage became less as the Battle progressed.

# CHAPTER VI

# THE
# COMMANDERS

**T**he outcome of the Battle of Britain would depend on several factors, all quantifiable—equipment, intelligence, the state of knowledge in electronics and radio. But another dimension to war, as to all human endeavor, is the nature of the individuals involved. Air Chief Marshal Sir Hugh Dowding and Reichsmarschall Hermann Goering could hardly have been more dissimilar. And on their differences depended much of the outcome of the Battle.

The eldest son of the founder of a preparatory school in Scotland, Hugh Dowding had had to set an example for the other boys. Duty, patriotism, good manners, and hard work were expected of him, and he fulfilled those requirements. A man of contrasts, he was quiet and intellectual, but a champion skier and polo player. Although a dedicated military man, he often offended higher authorities. Devoted to his goals, he often endangered them by not using the diplomacy that would have made those goals more easily won. Reserved and enigmatic, Dowding was no bookish sit-by-the-fire. He was attracted to flying, as he had been to skiing and polo, and learned to fly on his own time, through the Royal Aero Club. With the club's certificate he became eligible to join the Royal Flying Corps (RFC), and when World War I started, he served with the RFC in France. By the war's end, he had become a brigadier general.

Between the wars Dowding devoted himself to his work. His wife had died after two years of marriage, leaving him the responsibility of raising a son, who would later fly under his father's command in the Battle of Britain. Dowding dedicated himself totally to his work and remained a mystery, sometimes disliked or even feared because he could not tolerate those whom he thought fools. But he was generally respected, expecially by the men working most closely with him.

While serving on the Air Council, which advised Parliament on military aviation matters, Dowding was instrumental in the change from biplanes to monoplanes, and from wooden construction to metal. During his tenure on the Council as Member for Supply and Research, the first Hurricane and the prototype Spitfire flew. On his authority, research on radar was carried on, and he planned the tactics and ground-control system that would use the new device, which was not yet even completely designed.

In 1936 Fighter Command was organized, and the logical choice for its commander-in-chief was Hugh Dowding. It was his job to organize the fighter defense of Britain. Under his control were the fighters, the radar and ground-control network, the balloon barrage, and antiaircraft guns. He organized the Observer Corps, which would provide the vital information of the enemy's location once the planes were past the coastal radar.

Dowding was in no way a reckless man. The tactics of Fighter Command in the Battle of Britain were a direct reflection of his cool, logical mind. The German challenges did not tempt him to use one more fighter than necessary in any engagement. Dowding would weigh the glory of a big win one day against the long-range cost of losing aircraft and pilots. He forced the Germans to fight in British territory, where his coordinated ground-control system, better fuel

reserves, and the morale factor of defending their own turf gave the British advantages to balance the Germans' original superiority of numbers.

Cool and aloof, Dowding was not popular with many officials, including Winston Churchill, but his contributions to the success of Fighter Command in the Battle of Britain were enormous. And as important as technical and tactical contributions was Dowding's method of command. He delegated authority to his commanders and seldom interfered in their decisions. The morale of the pilots stayed high even during the darkest days of the Battle, when they were near exhaustion and most hard-pressed. They knew that their firsthand knowledge of the Battle and their opinions were respected— something the Luftwaffe pilots could not expect of their commander.

Hermann Goering was in most ways Dowding's opposite. Beyond their service as pilots in World War I, any similarity ended. Goering was a risk taker with no thought of the consequences. These were admirable qualities in a fighter pilot at that time, and they brought him fame and the command of Manfred von Richthofen's "Flying Circus" following the death of the great ace. Goering won the famous "Blue Max," the highest medal for meritorious service. In 1922 war hero Goering became a much-prized member of the Nazi party. The party badly needed respectable and admired members to counteract its image of being bullies and thugs. He moved up quickly in the party ranks to positions of power. His considerable personal charm was a fine mask for the man who

*Air Chief Marshal
Sir Hugh Dowding,
who commanded the
Royal Air Force in
the Battle of Britain*

helped organize the storm troopers, the Gestapo, and the first concentration camps.

Unlike the quiet, abstemious Dowding, Goering lived in a style few could equal. He had private hunting preserves, castles, the world's largest model-railway layout, and an art collection that grew as fast as he could steal the works from conquered nations and Jewish victims of Nazi pogroms. The overweight of the self-indulgent hedonist hid a man of great self-control. He had once been treated with morphine when wounded, and he had accidently become addicted. He cured himself—not an easy or a common thing. So he was called the Iron Man by his admirers, but Fat Man was a popular name with those not so fond of him.

Goering was a glory seeker, and so it was personally important to him that "his" Luftwaffe conquer Britain. He believed the theory that air bombardment could force an enemy to surrender, a theory that meant air power alone could win the war. Even if his fighters could not clear British skies of opposition, he was sure his bombers could force the British government to terms. He would consider this a personal victory.

Goering was a confidant of Hitler, who had benefited politically from the prestige that the World War I hero and his Luftwaffe had brought Germany in the early thirties. While Hitler usually thought in terms of a land army, he had seen the value of air power in the blitzkrieg. But the science of air war was as yet undeveloped. Hermann Goering's pursuit of glory led him to believe, and to convince Hitler, that

*Reichsmarschall*
*Hermann Goering,*
*commander of the*
*Luftwaffe, the*
*Nazi air force*

the mighty Luftwaffe could easily dominate the skies of Britain.

Fortunately for Britain, Goering's talents lay more in the direction of individual showmanship, both in his own life and in the way he ran his air force. Major German failings in the Battle of Britain were lack of coordination of information, of technology, and of purpose. The German pilots and their immediate commanders knew that the British were holding their own in numbers of planes launched and in numbers of kills. They knew the British could nearly always find them. It should have been obvious that British aircraft production and pilot training were better than German estimate and that the radar stations should be important targets. But the significance of these facts was never assimilated in Berlin. There the generals and admirals argued over strategy based on limited and often incorrect information and fought their jealous battles over the value of their respective services in the war effort.

Most telling, perhaps, was the lack of unity of purpose. With invasion planned for September 15, 1940, when the Luftwaffe expected to have won control of the skies, the actual organization of an invasion fleet should never have been postposed until July 31. And the preparations that were made were surprisingly inadequate. For example, the Germans had commandeered French, Dutch, and Belgian unarmored barges and small boats, whose crews were of those same nationalities. They surely would not support the effort of a German invasion with any enthusiasm.

The key difference between the opposing forces seems to lie then in their professionalism. In short, the British knew what they were doing and the Germans did not.

# CHAPTER VII

## THE
## BATTLE

**G**ermany's overall objective in the Battle of Britain was to gain control of British air space. This was an absolute requirement for the planned invasion that would give Germany control of the land below. But the Germans would discover that the British control of that land and direction of their fighters from the ground-control centers was a decisive factor in the Battle.

The Battle developed in four phases. First came the *Kanalkampf*—the Channel War—attacks on British shipping in the Channel, where the Germans hoped to draw the RAF into battle. There, rather than over British countryside, the Germans felt that the British would lose enough planes and pilots to destroy their air-defense capability. These attacks lasted for most of July 1940 and into August. Unfortunately for them, the Germans learned that the RAF would not commit large numbers of planes to protect shipping.

The second stage of the battle, *Adlerangriff* (Eagle Attack), was intended to destroy British radar, airfields, and aircraft production, so weakening the RAF that the Luftwaffe could begin reducing the British resistance. *Adlerangriff* began on August 13, 1940, and in spite of a week-long effort, seemed to have little success.

The third stage concentrated attacks primarily on the airfields in southeast England from which the RAF so effectively launched its defensive fighters and to which they returned for fuel, maintenance, and fresh pilots. After two weeks, however, the Germans turned their attention elsewhere.

In the fourth stage they attacked London. Although the capital had previously been off-limits, the change in strategy came about on the theory that destruction in the city would so damage morale and disrupt the government that capitulation would follow.

Why, despite superior numbers, recent experience in air combat, and the high morale resulting from the successful blitzkrieg, did the Luftwaffe fail in each stage? And why did the high command not recognize the reasons behind their overall failure and adopt a different strategy? The answer lies somewhere beyond numbers, experience, and previous successes.

The *Kanalkampf* presented Britain with a two-sided problem. If the RAF made an all-out effort to stop German attacks on British ships, it would surely lose many planes and pilots before a main attack on England began. If the RAF held back, the Germans might effectively control Channel shipping.

Meeting the Germans over the Channel had some other disadvantages for the British. When the Luftwaffe and the RAF met over the Channel, British radar was not as effective there as over land. The Luftwaffe could take off, reach altitude, and form up farther inland in France and out of range of the British radar stations. Already at combat altitude, the Germans could cross the Channel in five minutes after being detected by radar. A Spitfire needed twenty minutes to reach an effective combat altitude, so a longer warning was essential.

Air Chief Marshal Dowding, head of Fighter Command, was a veteran of long military experience. He possessed the ability to make decisions that took into account the long-term problem and that might not be immediately popular with some people. Instead of sending up large numbers of fighters to defend British shipping, he held back as many as he could for those more dangerous attacks on land targets. This decision had also preserved British pilots, who were still in short supply in spite of the stepped-up training efforts.

The weather, for once, favored the British. A rainy July inhibited German efforts to find the convoys. Nevertheless, there was enough activity for each side to begin to take the measure of the other.

The British learned, for example, how sturdy the German bombers were. Squadron Commander Peter Townsend, in a Hurricane, attacked a German bomber, a Dornier 17. The German plane made it back to base in spite of 220 bullets in it. The all-metal Dornier had armor protection and some duplication of systems as a backup in case of damage. It also had self-sealing fuel tanks, constructed in three layers. When pierced, the center layer, made of crude rubber, swelled up and filled the hole. This relatively simple device brought many bombers home. The British had thought such fuel tanks unnecessary at first, but by the beginning of the Battle most of their fighters had been equipped in the same manner.

The German attacks on shipping included dropping magnetic mines in the major approaches to ports, the Thames and Humber estuaries and the Firth of Forth. They also attacked factories in widely scattered locations and experimented with their own radio guidance system in night bombing sorties.

The first phase of the Battle had many experiments. The pilots were learning the capabilities of their own planes and the quality of the enemy pilots, and developing the most effective tactics of aerial combat. Air war had no precedents; they had to make their own rules.

Most successful pilots had the courage to fly very close to the enemy, assuring hits. But courage could not be enough. They had to aim their guns while both their own and the enemy plane moved at three hundred to four hundred miles per hour. To assess the size and speed of the enemy and the distance and angle between the two aircraft required instant decisions. During the Battle of Britain, gunsights were still very primitive, so the pilots had to depend more on their own judgment. Even an excellent pilot might not have the necessary ability as a marksman to become an ace.

The British planes used a variety of bullets: normal, armor-piercing, and incendiary. The incendiary bullets proved very useful in an unexpected way. Upon striking the target they made a bright yellow flash, which gave the attacking pilot the useful information that he was aiming correctly. Instead of having to cover a broad area, he could concentrate his fire.

The pilots also relearned an old military maxim: the advantage goes with surprise attack. In aerial combat this meant having superior altitude and attacking with the sun at one's back and in the enemy's eyes. Visibility was paramount, and achieving the necessary amount of visibility required more than altitude and hiding in the blinding sunlight. Canopy design affects visibility, and the Spitfire had the advantage there. A less obvious but also important factor in visibility was the design of helmets, oxygen masks, and wires for earphones and microphones. These and the life vests, called "Mae Wests," could become entangled, restricting the movement of the pilot's head.

As the pilots learned the ways of aerial combat, the ground-control system became more and more efficient. The controllers' ability to judge the altitude, course, and distance of the enemy improved. And although some pilots objected to being directed from the ground, the system constituted the RAF's principal advantage over the Luftwaffe.

The British ability to build and to repair aircraft was also tested during the first phase of the Battle. This ability included salvaging the planes—German and British—that could not be repaired, melting them down, and using the metal in building new machines. The Civilian Repair Organization—the CRO—used specially designed trailers to transport the downed fighter planes from the fields into which they fell.

The CRO had been created by the minister of aircraft production, Lord Beaverbrook, a Canadian maverick. He was not well liked by the Air Ministry, which resented his unorthodox tactics. But "the Beaver" knew what was needed and how to get it done. As minister of aircraft production, he felt that all aircraft in storage should be under his control, as were those being built or repaired. When the Air Ministry objected, the Beaver shocked everyone by padlocking the storage hangars. He did not wait for the Air Ministry to find out and inform him, through official channels, of necessary replacements. His own son, a squadron leader, and Group Commander Park, of 11 Group, stayed in personal contact with him, and Beaverbrook immediately supplied whatever they found any squadron needed, without consulting the Air Ministry.

Beaverbrook did not tolerate the age-old military problem of supply personnel hoarding spare equipment against nebulous future use. He would raid the squadrons for excess parts to deliver to the production lines. In a sense he also "raided" the business world, commissioning, and seldom paying, experts from other industries to solve problems in the aircraft industry. The CRO had such success that, of all the aircraft supplied to Fighter Command during the Battle, one-third was returned to battle from repair units. And Beaverbrook even set up a repair service into which a pilot might fly his damaged aircraft to be repaired while he waited. Aircraft supplied to the squadrons in July were more than enough to replace those planes lost. The whole month's count of losses equaled about a week's production.

Pilots were not so easily replaced. July was a period of relatively light fighting, and still, many experienced pilots had been wounded or killed. By the end of the month, only about half of the pilots had had combat experience. Weather and German bombing raids had interfered with training. Rotation of pilots to noncombat duty for a rest was impossible due to the limited numbers of pilots available. In fact, there were days when a pilot would fight, land for repairs or fuel, and return to the battle a second and third time. Some crash-landed in a distant field and then returned to their air base to fly again that day. The Battle had not yet reached its critical phase, and fatigue had already become a real hazard. The Luftwaffe, on the other hand, had an ample supply of pilots and crews.

But the Luftwaffe had very poor information about the supply of British pilots and aircraft. Because the British did not respond to German raids in large numbers, the German command assumed that there was a severe shortage of both, and that it would not take long for attrition to give the Germans the victory. The pilots on both sides tended to overestimate their "kills." This was often impossible to avoid, but the problem was worse with the German reporting. Any pilot exaggeration was nothing compared to that at the various levels of command up to Reichsmarschall Goering. He only wanted to hear the good news, and he certainly added to the inflation of numbers as he passed information on to Hitler.

Such confusion occurred in other areas of German command. If the RAF had a pilot shortage, the Germans had a shortage of accurate information. With too many channels for information to be fed through, the men in decision-making positions had difficulty acting effectively. The confusion led to waste in manpower and supplies, and missed opportunities, because responsibilities were not clearly designated.

The Germans also seriously misunderstood the British radar and ground systems. They never realized the vital importance of the Chain Home system. They thought the British squadrons came under the local control of individual stations, instead of under a central control. Had this been true, each squadron would have been limited to use in a certain area, rather than flexible enough to be sent where the fighting was. Because of this misunderstanding, the Germans delayed attempts on radar stations until the preparatory attacks for *Adlerangriff*. At that time they damaged three stations and rendered one inoperative for several days. However, the British sent fake signals from that point to disguise the gap. The Germans did not pursue this small success, because they did not realize that it was a success.

At the end of the *Kanalkampf*, the first stage of the Battle, the RAF had lost seventy and the Germans one hundred eighty aircraft. More than half of the German losses were the more vulnerable bombers, making the fighter losses on both sides similar. The British learned how important was the accuracy of their radar operators and the judgments made by the controllers and group commanders. Without these, all the skill and courage of the pilots could not have prevailed, for early warning was essential if the British planes were to be at the right place and altitude and in the right numbers to meet the enemy.

The Germans were still suffering heavy losses of their bombers and had to determine how to give them protection without heavy losses of fighters. The British would concentrate on the bombers, but when engaged by the fighters, were a match for them. Dowding's policy of not sending up huge numbers of planes paid off both by not losing more than necessary and by deceiving the Germans as to the real strength of Fighter Command. The Germans consistently underestimated the numbers of British fighters.

This deception was compounded by the Germans' optimistic view of winning the Battle in a short time. The higher up the German chain of command information went, the more inflated became the estimates of German strength compared to British. The professionalism of the Luftwaffe command did not compare to the British in either cooperation among the various units or in agreement on tactics. The commander of the Luftwaffe, Reichsmarschall Goering, was concerned more with the personal glory he would receive if Britain were subjugated by air power alone than he was with the details of how it would be done. He ran much of the Battle from Karinhall, his country estate. Air Marshal Dowding, in contrast, remained in close contact and in personal control of Fighter Command.

As a result of the weaknesses in the Luftwaffe's higher command, *Adlerangriff*, the second stage, commenced with no overall strategy and too little information on which to base one. Their target information was incomplete; consequently, the Germans destroyed less important airfields, used for auxiliary operations, and the British quickly repaired the damage. They night-bombed the few aircraft factories whose locations they knew, using directional radio beams from the Continent. But the British devised ways of jamming the beams. And the Germans did not know the locations of many of the aircraft factories. Although they made heavy raids on the docks at the port of Liverpool and on Birmingham, an industrial center, they still did not understand the essential role of the radar stations in British deployment of aircraft.

The score at the end of August 13, the day *Adlerangriff* began, was 1,485 sorties flown by the Luftwaffe that day, twice the number flown by the RAF. German losses were forty-five aircraft. The British lost thirteen, and recovered six of their pilots. Two days later, August 15, occurred the heaviest fighting of the Battle of Britain. The Luftwaffe flew 1,786 sorties, this time committing 1,266 fighters to protect 520 bombers. The RAF lost thirty-four planes to air combat, and the Germans lost seventy-five. The Luftwaffe referred to this day as Black Thursday.

On August 16 the Germans pressed the attack, but the cloudy weather interfered, and losses on both sides were lower. The next day they launched almost as many flights as on August 15, but this time German losses were proportionately higher than the British—seventy-one to twenty-seven. Poor weather for the next five days ended *Adlerangriff.*

Goering was becoming concerned, and for good reason. The German losses were heavy, and British resistance was not collapsing as he had hoped. The British consistently attacked the bombers and avoided engaging the German fighters whenever possible. Goering ordered heavier fighter protection as well as directing the fighters to stay closer to the bombers. Without their altitude, the exposed fighters lost one of their advantages.

Goering made the serious error of questioning the importance of the radar stations. Another mistake was underestimating RAF strength. Goering thought that the British were not replacing lost aircraft and that they would eventually lose by attrition.

On August 24 the weather improved, and from that time until September 6, the Luftwaffe made heavy daytime bombing raids on the airfields in southeast England. These fields lay within the fuel range of the Me 109s so they could function as bomber escorts. For the first time, British fighter losses were heavier than German losses. Total losses for the British of 290 planes to 380 for the Germans was the most favorable ratio to date for the Luftwaffe.

Despite these heavy losses, Fighter Command's problem was not the number of planes. During this time the British lost ten percent of their pilots per week. The experienced pilots were near exhaustion, and the new ones were barely trained. Their training period had been cut to two weeks—two weeks to learn to fly before going into battle. The course had originally been six months long. And the higher-ranking pilots—squadron commanders—were also short on experience. Some had no combat time at all, and one had never flown a Hurricane—the plane in which he was to lead his squadron to battle.

The attacks on the British airfields brought the war to the support groups. The mechanics, WAAFs, civilian maintenance personnel, all acted for the most part with bravery. The vital operations room at one base was damaged, breaking communications with the central control station. The engineers who worked to repair the damage did so next to an unexploded bomb.

One German bomber, off course, dropped its bombs on London, giving the civilian population a taste of worse to come. The British launched a retaliatory raid on Berlin. The actual damage was small, but the shock to the Germans was huge. They had felt that they were at a safe distance from the fighting. But the bombing of strictly civilian targets was gaining acceptance and would increase on both sides.

*A German Me 109 chases a British
Spitfire over English territory
during the Battle of Britain.*

On September 7 the Germans made a major tactical change—and blundered. The RAF was under terrible strain due to loss of pilots and damage to airfields. Bomb raids on aircraft factories were just beginning to threaten the supply of replacement aircraft. Had the Germans pressed the advantage, they might have accomplished their aim of gaining control of the air over England. But they did not. They decided to concentrate on the bombing of London. The British had a breathing space to repair airfields and the factories they needed to supply the large numbers of aircraft to replenish the squadrons. To understand why the Germans switched objectives, it is necessary to look at the situation from their point of view.

Invasion—or so clear a threat of invasion that the British would come to terms—was the ultimate German goal. That invasion, code-named Sea Lion, had to take place before the autumn weather turned foul and air cover could not be provided for the invasion force. Even with exaggerated estimates of "failing" British strength, the Germans decided that they could not expect to gain air superiority with the current tactics in time to launch Sea Lion.

Also, the British bombing raids on Berlin, on August 28, 30, and 31, had been a blow to German morale that called for retaliation. Hitler decided to bomb the British capital city. The intent was to destroy the dock facilities, industrial areas, and supply depots and sources. Above all, the Germans thought it was sure to destroy morale, which would hasten the end of the war. On September 5 and 6 they made night bombing raids, and on the seventh, they made the first daylight attacks. Huge fires started that burned on into the darkness and lit the way for more bombers. The attacks continued as the weather permitted, but while losses were painful, the damage had no strategic significance. Repairs to railroad facilities were prompt. No critical losses occurred in the burning of storage facilities. Civilian morale did not crack. Indeed, the Londoners upheld the British reputation of doing best with their backs to the wall.

But the information that the Germans received from friendly sources in London or by relay from their embassy in Washington was that the center of London was devastated, the people weary and pessimistic, and capitulation near. Goering decided to press the attack on the city. Hitler began a final evaluation of the possibilities for invasion. Operation Sea Lion was not going to be ready to launch until early October when there would be only a week or two of good weather left in which to make the crossing. After that the autumn storms and mists would roll in. Or, perhaps by then, the British resistance, weakened by the bombing, would be so low that the invasion might not be necessary.

The bombing of London continued day and night. Spells of bad weather prevented the British fighters from meeting some of the raids, and German intelligence optimistically predicted the RAF was nearly out of planes and pilots. But on the next raid, the German pilots would find the British massed to meet them. "Here come the 'last fifty' Spitfires," was the bitter comment they would make. Their intelligence service had been wrong again.

These experiences did not persuade the German high command that it should reassess its plans. On September 15, it made a mass daylight bombing raid. Over two hundred bombers with heavy fighter escort launched for London. Another seventy bombers with escort were dispatched for Portsmouth to divert some of the British fighters from the larger attack. In an effort to convince the British that they could amass such power time and time again, the Germans committed nearly all their bombers and fighters.

Nearly two hundred Hurricanes and Spitfires met them over London. This was many more than the Germans had anticipated, and that finally convinced the Luftwaffe that British strength was far higher than their reports indicated. Those Londoners not in their air-raid shelters could follow the battles, as the Spitfires and Me 109s met in the cold, thin air at twenty thousand feet, marking their crisscrossed paths with condensation trails. The Hurricanes did their job of attacking

*A pilot's view of London ablaze
after German bombing*

the bombers and broke up the formation. The bombs were dumped all over the city, but very few hit their intended, strategically important targets. The bombers had been harried by the British all the way in from the coast and were under continuous attack as they headed home without their fuel-short fighter escort. Luftwaffe losses are still not precisely known but were approximately fifty-five to the RAF's twenty-six lost.

This was discouraging news for the Germans. The British still had command of their own sky and their Bomber Command was making raids on the French ports where the Germans were assembling an invasion fleet. The German bombers continued their raids and were always met by the British in apparently undiminished numbers. The German estimate of British strength was still fatally low—five hundred pilots and five hundred planes. In fact, at the end of September there were 732 pilots and 1,581 fighters. And this number indicated not only that the numbers were larger than estimated, but that, in contrast to German expectations, those numbers were increasing. Instead of the attrition they had expected and blindly insisted was occurring, the Germans were actually facing a more heavily armed foe than at the beginning of the Battle.

The Luftwaffe, in contrast, had dropped from its initial strength of 950 fighters to 600 and from 1,000 bombers to 800. Major General von Waldau, the operations officer of Luftwaffe Command, said, "Our air strength by next spring will at best have regained the level held at the beginning of the air war against England. We would need four times that strength to force Britain to surrender." The production rate of German aircraft was far lower than that of the British. Von Waldau, who knew that Hitler was planning to attack Russia, added, "Two-front war cannot be sustained."

September 15 is celebrated as Battle of Britain Day, although it was not the highest-scoring day for the British (German losses had been greater on August 15 and 18). But on September 15 the Germans were finally convinced that they could not break the British will to resist, nor could they expect a speedy defeat of the RAF. In the Battle of Britain, the first and only exclusively *air* battle, the British had not won—but they had not lost. And that was most important. There would be more battles in the air over Britain. But the Germans had given up the invasion plans—Operation Sea Lion was cancelled.

# CHAPTER VIII

## THE
## PEOPLE
## AT
## WAR

**A**fter the betrayal of Czechoslovakia, September 30, 1938, British public opinion clearly changed. In the time between that event and the invasion of Poland on September 1, 1939, the people came to recognize the nature of Nazi policy and the inevitability of war. When Britain declared war on September 3, plans had already been made for the evacuation of children from the major cities to the country. Most parents saw this as a wise move and accepted the government-sponsored program.

In early September families had begun queuing up at train stations and other pickup points. Hundreds of children were herded along by schoolteachers and scoutmasters, each child wearing an identification tag and carrying a gas mask and a bundle with towel, underwear, and toothbrush. Some were clearly afraid, but only a few cried. Many seemed to think of it as an adventure.

Perhaps middle-class children looked on trips to the country as holiday outings, but the little Cockneys from the East End had seldom left the city. What adults might see as a welcome relief from urban crowding and dirt, these slum children often found lonely and threatening. They had seldom been out of range of human contact in the city. Here they could find themselves out of touching, and even shouting, distance of another person. And their slum ways, the result of

*Children in London's East End prepare*
*for evacuation during the fighting.*

minimal bathing and sanitary facilities, and the lice they brought with them were not welcome in the neat village homes. There were painful adjustments to make—by guests and hosts. But they coped, and in fact, many formed lifelong attachments. They had in common human needs and fears, and a common heritage. Most differences disappeared between adult and child; country- and city-bred; upper-, middle-, and lower-class people. They were, above all, British.

Nearly two million children were evacuated over a two-year period, along with some mothers of infants, pregnant women, the elderly, and invalids. The parents who saw their children off were aware how long this might last and what their own risks were in the urban target areas. But with a sense of relief that their children would be safer, the adults turned to their task—getting ready to go to war.

December of 1939 was especially quiet for Christmas shoppers. Very few children were seen lining up to shake hands with Father Christmas, and acceptance of the inevitability of attack was apparent in the changing city scene.

The cities prepared for bombing raids. Prefabricated bomb shelters, of dubious value, were distributed; trenches were dug in the parks; sandbags were piled everywhere. In the sky silvery barrage balloons held up steel cables to discourage low-flying enemy aircraft. Air-raid warnings were sounded, some as practice and some in response to single German planes flying reconnaisance missions. Posters were pasted up everywhere with advice and warnings of what to do in an air raid (seek shelter, do not impede firemen, etc.), what to do in case of invasion (stay put, do not block the road, you will be in danger of being strafed, and you will impede your own troops' movement toward the enemy), and what to keep silent about (your factory's munitions production, where your son or husband's military unit was stationed, what ships were sailing). In the countryside, home-defense units prepared to receive the enemy with everything from World War I weapons to pitchforks.

To avoid giving information to the enemy, there was a

blackout on news, which frustrated the ordinary citizen, who thus probably knew less than the Germans did. The long wait from September 1939 until April 1940, the "Phony War," was full of frustrations. Gas rationing was accepted as necessary, but the restriction on travel was uncomfortable. For a while the theaters were closed. One newspaper columnist said of the lull, "The public at the moment is feeling like a little boy who stuffs his fingers in his ears on Fourth of July only to discover that the cannon cracker has not gone off after all." She added, "Boredom is nearly as potent a menace as bombs." That, of course, was before the bombs fell.

Meanwhile it was off to military training for the young men and off to the offices and factories for everyone else. Women took the places left in factories by men leaving for military service, and women did military duty as well. They were valuable links in the ground-control system as they operated radar equipment, did observation duty, and used the resulting information to plot positions of friend and enemy on the map tables at Fighter Command Headquarters and Sector operations rooms.

From the "miracle" of Dunkirk, when the civilian sailors had made an enormous contribution to the rescue of the British Expeditionary Force, the British public was in the war with a will. When the "Phony War" became a real one, it was literally in their own front yard. They watched the battles in the sky over their homes while listening to radio reports that were like sporting events. But they knew full well that the "players" brought down were likely to die. And, eventually, the onlookers were in this deadly game themselves.

In September 1940 the Germans began the long-expected bombing of London. The changed strategy brought vital relief to the RAF. The bombed airfields could be repaired and the dangerously low supply of fighters could be replenished. But the people of London would suffer terribly.

Legend has it that the people of Britain were staunch and fearless, putting their strength without question into the war effort, never losing their belief in ultimate victory. The truth is that they were as varied as human beings everywhere. They understood that the war threatened England, the center of a world empire and the oldest surviving democracy. But those are concepts. The everyday reality was that someone might drop a bomb that would kill loved ones and obliterate one's home. And another reality brought home to the slum dwellers of the East End was that bomb targets seemed closely related to class differences.

The East End was a factory and warehouse district as well as the location of the docks of Britain's largest port. Here cars, tanks, and trucks were manufactured; here food was stored; here the mills had turned out cloth since the industrial revolution—in the same buildings that were nearly a century old. Next to these were the tenements that were nearly as old, and dry as tinder waiting to be lit.

When the first bombs fell on the East End, a holocaust erupted and with it the anger of the slum dwellers. Driven from their homes, the ones who had had so little now had nothing. They crowded for shelter in the subway stations until conditions became so intolerable a local police chief described it as being "like a painting of hell." The crowds of people on the subway platforms were afraid to leave, prefer- ring the sickening smell of the ill and unwashed and the cramped conditions to the fearsome conditions above ground.

In contrast, the areas where the more affluent lived were hardly touched. There was no reason to bomb apartment houses, department stores and parks.

Soldiers whose families lived in the East End were get- ting no news from home and the rumors made things sound even worse than they were. Many of the men deserted or went absent without leave to find out how their families fared.

The anger of the East Enders at the lack of assistance they received in these first heavy bombing raids was further fueled by communist agitators. Two of them, Phil Piraten and Tubby Rosen, were saying that this was a "bosses' war" and that the East Enders were victims of a capitalist plot. They led a march to the Savoy Hotel, a luxury establishment popular with government ministers, the nobility, and newspaper reporters. The hotel had an air raid shelter that was relatively spacious, where regular guests had reserved bunks.

The slum dwellers poured into the lobby, alarming the staff by their presence, but not causing any damage. A frantic employee who called the police was told that, as a hotel, they were required to serve bona fide travelers and "These look like bona fide travelers to me. Now if they make a row, we'll be willing to escort them out."

In a particularly English gesture, the manager offered to serve the "travelers" tea. The leaders realized they had made a mistake not timing the march for the evening hours when the swank clientele would have been present. Had they done that, the marchers would have shared the shelters with them and made a bigger impression.

The anger of the East Enders was alleviated when the bombing became wider spread. When bombs hit the central city and the affluent West End, the middle and upper classes were finally in the same situation. And when one bomb fell on Buckingham Palace, they were all finally in it together. In the East End, Tubby Rosen canceled a planned march on the palace, saying, "I don't feel so bad now that George and his flunkies are getting it, too."

But most of the people found that being in this together helped them endure. The queen said, "I can finally look the East Enders in the face." When she was asked if she and the princesses Elizabeth and Margaret would go to Canada for safety, she replied, "The children will not leave unless I do. I shall not leave unless their father does, and the King will not leave the country in any circumstances whatsoever." Churchill recognized the importance of this as a morale factor and ordered the newspapers to tell the story: "Let the humble people of England know that they are not alone and that the King and Queen are sharing it with them."

As the night bombing raids became more frequent, Lon-

doners queued up outside the bomb shelters every afternoon. They carried blankets, suitcases, books—whatever would help pass the night. The shelters in subways and store basements had little or no furniture, so people of all ages slept on the concrete floors. Members of the Women's Volunteer Service served tea and other refreshments and did first-aid work.

The people in the shelters became quite friendly. Dart games and sing-alongs kept spirits up and passed time while overhead the nightly raids took their toll and the firemen, police, air-raid wardens, and rescue workers went about their grim business.

Digging out victims from the rubble took hours, sometimes days. The rescuers were often construction workers who had some understanding of the structures that had been destroyed. They would not give up as long as they thought anyone might still be alive, and for a child they would be especially determined. Dogs and even human beings acted as "sniffers," smelling blood and pointing out the probable places to look. Some of the human "sniffers" could tell by the scent if the victim were alive.

Particularly hazardous duty was done by the military demolition teams, which risked their lives defusing unexploded bombs. Some of the bombs had simply malfunctioned but might go off if mishandled. Some were dropped with parachutes and would hang up on trees or lampposts, where a touch could set them off.

In the daytime most people tried to go about their business as usual. Windowless shops and restaurants continued

*Londoners found shelter in stations of the Underground during the Battle of Britain.*

to function, and people who had slept, or attempted to sleep, on shelter floors would still go to work the next day. The theaters were crowded, although their hours were earlier than in peacetime so the show would be over before the air raids began. Sometimes the raids beat the last curtain, and the audience would stay for the end of the show. The performers believed in the tradition that the show must go on—and the theatergoers of London obviously agreed.

The government created or encouraged morale-building activities, whether it was movies glorifying English heroes from history, simple adventure movies about the war, or radio shows with corny jokes about the war, the inconveniences, or the enemy. People welcomed every opportunity to escape for a moment the nightly horror of the raids. And morale improved as the government became better organized to provide shelters and food for the homeless. But perhaps the strongest factor was universal admiration for the Royal Air Force.

The gallant few—a thousand pilots—were from all classes and many nations. The British were joined by pilots from the dominions of Canada, Australia, and New Zealand. There was a squadron of Polish pilots who had escaped the Nazis. Czechs, French, Dutch, Norwegians joined them to fight the common enemy. And there were Americans there as well. All fought as if it were their homeland below. And it was, in a sense, their own homes they fought for. If the Nazis could not win here over Britain, they could eventually be beaten.

# CHAPTER IX

# THE
# TURNING
# POINT

**T**he German advance had spread across Europe unchecked until it broke on the rocky shores of Britain. After the Battle of Britain, Germany still controlled Europe from the Balkans to the Atlantic and from Norway to the Mediterranean. The failure of the German plans to destroy the RAF and invade was, of course, important to the British. But why was the Battle a crucial turning point, perhaps *the* turning point, in a war that had just begun?

First: an invasion that did not succeed when Britain was critically weak after Dunkirk was far less likely to succeed after the British spent the winter of 1940–41 strengthening their defenses. What the Germans had seen as a short war was now sure to last another year or two at least. And their strategy had been designed for a short war.

Second: the Luftwaffe was weakened by its losses of men and equipment. Its inherent weaknesses were exposed and never corrected. The Germans did not develop the long-range fighter needed for the enormous areas soon to be involved—Russia, North Africa, the Mediterranean, the Balkans. They never built a heavier bomber that could carry larger bombloads, and they did not correct the central flaws of organization—intelligence, communication, and ground control. Even if these weaknesses had been recognized, the Battle of Britain kept the Germans busy until they were too involved in the widening conflict to make the needed improvements.

Third: the British holding action convinced the United States that Britain would be a strong ally rather than the liability that many had predicted. American popular support for the Allied cause grew, and American aid increased.

Fourth: a secure Britain became the vital air and naval base and the launching point for the Allied counterattack, first by British and American bombers and eventually by the enormous forces gathered for the Normandy invasion of D-Day, June 6, 1944.

In these two crucial months, August and September 1940, the course of World War II was established. The Thousand-Year Reich proclaimed by Hitler would last less than five more years. A determined people made a stand, led by a doughty old man with a gift of oratory and a vision of history and the future that inspired them. And that man, Winston Churchill, could say of the young men who defended them the words that still hold true:

Never in the field of human conflict was so much owed by so many to so few.

# FOR FURTHER READING

Churchill, Winston S. *The Gathering Storm*. Boston: Houghton Mifflin Co., 1948.

_____. *Their Finest Hour*. Boston: Houghton Mifflin Co., 1949.

Deighton, Len. *Blitzkrieg*. New York: Alfred A. Knopf, 1980.

_____. *Fighter*. New York: Alfred A. Knopf, 1978.

Gilbert, Felix. *The End of the European Era*. New York: W.W. Norton & Co., 1979.

Lash, Joseph P. *Roosevelt and Churchill*. New York: W.W. Norton & Co., 1976.

Mosley, Leonard. *Backs to the Wall*. New York: Random House, 1971.

Reader's Digest Editors. *Illustrated Story of World War II*. Pleasantville, N.Y.: The Reader's Digest Association, 1969.

Shirer, William L. *Berlin Diary*. New York: Alfred A. Knopf, 1941.

Smith, Gaddis. *American Diplomacy During the Second World War*. New York: John Wiley and Sons, 1965.

Sontag, Raymond S. *A Broken World*. New York: Harper & Row, 1971.

Taylor, Telford. *The Breaking Wave*. New York: Simon & Schuster, 1967.

Watt, Richard M. *The Kings Depart*. New York: Simon & Schuster, 1968.

Wernick, Robert and the editors of Time-Life books. *Blitz-krieg.* New York: Time-Life Books, 1976.

_____. *Battle of Britain.* New York: Time-Life Books, 1976.

Wilson, Harold. *A Prime Minister on Prime Ministers.* New York: Summit Books, 1977.

# INDEX

Italy *(continued)*
man alliance, 23, 25, 26, 28; and Spain, 5, 25, 26

*Kanalkampf,* 74, 75, 80

League of Nations, 15, 17, 22, 23, 24, 25
Locarno, Treaty of, 24, 35
London, air raids, 75–82, 84–87, 92, 93–98
*Luftwaffe:* and Battle of Britain strategy, 70, 72, 74–75, 76, 79, 80–81; *Adlerangriff,* 79, 80, 81; *Kanalkampf,* 74, 75, 80, Sea Lion, 84, 85, 88; command, 69–72, 75, 79, 80; Condor Legion, 26–27, 50; Dunkirk, 1, 2; information failure, 74, 75, 79, 80, 85, 87; losses, 80, 81, 82, 87–88, 100; plane design, 62–63; weaknesses, 79, 80–81, 100

Marx, Karl, 10
ME *109,* 18, 62–63, 82, *83,* 85
Messerschmitt, Willy, 62
Mitchell, Reginald, 60
Mussolini, Benito, 22, 25, 26, 28

Nazism: Austria, 29, 30; Czechoslovakia, 30, 31, 32; Germany, 8–12, 16, 19
Netherlands, 1, 44, 45, 46
Norway, 1, 43, 44

Pacifist movement, British, 13–16, 17, 24, 30, 32, 39
Papen, Franz von, 10
"Phony War," 41, 42, 93
Poland, 1, 5, 23, 41, 43, 90

Radar system, British, 51–56, 67, 72, 75, 79, 80, 81, 82, 93
Richthoven, Manfred von, 69
Royal Air Force: and *Adlerangriff,* 74, 81, 82; air war, tactics, 74, 76–77, 78; and CRO, 77–78; Fighter Command, 53, 54, *55,* 67–69, 75, 76, 78, 80, 82; ground control system, 51–57, 67, 74, 77, 79, 80, 82, 93; and *Kanalkampf,* 80; losses, 78–79, 80, 81, 82, 84; multinational pilots, 98; plane design, 18, 60–63, 67
Russia: and Britain, 40, 41; and Czechoslovakia, 30, 31, 40; and Finland, 43; and Germany, 16, 40, 41, 43, 87; and Spain, 26

Schuschnigg, Kurt von, 25
Sea Lion, 84, 85, 88
Sinclair, Archibald, 34
Spain, Civil War, 5, 25–27, 29, 50
Spitfires, 18, 38, 60, 62, 63, 67, 75, 77, *83,* 85
Stalin, Joseph, 41
Stukas, 2, 3, 23
Sudetenland, 29–32, 39

Ultra operation, 56
United States, 23, 40, 101

Versailles Treaty, 4–5, 10, 15, 16, 19, 24, 29, 35
Waldau, General von, 87
Watson-Watt, Robert, 51
Wilson, Harold, 28, 34–35
Wilson, Horace, 28
World War I, 4–5, 8, 9, 13, 50